MURDER & MAYHEM
— IN —
TOMBSTONE

MURDER & MAYHEM
— IN —
TOMBSTONE

CODY POLSTON

THE
History
PRESS

Published by The History Press
Charleston, SC
www.historypress.com

First published 2024

Manufactured in the United States

ISBN 9781467156516

Library of Congress Control Number: 2023950476

Notice: The information in this book is true and complete to the best of our knowledge. It is offered without guarantee on the part of the author or The History Press. The author and The History Press disclaim all liability in connection with the use of this book.

CONTENTS

INTRODUCTION

The expanse of land in the southeast corner of Arizona was one of the last to be populated by settlers heading west. It was home to numerous fierce Apache tribes, and when Cochise passed away in 1874, no clear leader succeeded him. This caused many Apache to become even more hostile, creating a considerable risk for any settlers who dared to venture near this region.

Due to the San Pedro Valley's sparse population and remoteness, Ed Schieffelin decided to prospect there in 1877. After many months of working the hills east of the San Pedro River, he found pieces of silver ore in a dry wash on a high plateau called Goose Flats. It took him several more months to locate the source. When he found the vein, he calculated it to be fifty feet long and twelve inches wide. Schieffelin's legal mining claim was sited near Scott Lenox's grave site, and on September 21, 1877, Schieffelin filed his first claim and, logically, named his stake Tombstone. The name came to mean much more for those notorious and nameless individuals who died there and are laid to rest in Boothill.

The initial claims were filed, and the population of Watervale, near the Lucky Cuss mine, grew to about one hundred. Edward Schieffelin, his brother Al and Richard Gird, their mining engineer partner, had found two impressive ore deposits—the Toughnut and the Lucky Cuss. They also owned a part of Hank Williams's Grand Central, which they named the Contention. This caused the San Pedro Valley to become a booming place for prospectors.

A welcome sign for Tombstone in the 1940s. *Library of Congress.*

It was ironic that the American Western dream of striking silver almost overnight was contradicted by hard-rock mining. You needed plenty of money and a lot of organization to get the ore out. Anson P.K. Safford, an ex-governor of the territory, offered to raise enough funds to purchase a share in the strike, so the Tombstone Mining and Milling Company was formed to construct a stamping mill.

Construction had already begun on the mill when U.S. deputy mineral surveyor Solon M. Allis revealed his survey of the townsite on March 5, 1879. The tents and shacks near the Lucky Cuss were moved to the new townsite on Goose Flats, a mesa above the Toughnut Mine broad enough to hold a growing town. Lots were sold on Allen Street for five dollars each. The town rapidly grew to some forty cabins and just over one hundred residents. At the town's official founding in March 1879, it took its name from Schieffelin's first mining claim. By fall 1879, several thousand souls lived in a canvas-and-matchstick camp perched above the richest silver strike in the Arizona Territory.

Tombstone was no different than any other mining town; the mill and mines worked 24/7 in three shifts, and miners earned a good wage of four dollars per day. Consequently, young men without families had extra cash and needed somewhere to blow off steam. Allen Street was the perfect spot for them to do just that.

Nearly 110 locations were licensed to sell liquor, and most sold other things, too. The hotels, saloons, gambling dens, dance halls and brothels were open twenty-four hours a day. Though the historical records of this era are incomplete, confrontations between individuals inevitably happened for the same reasons they do today, with roughly 40 percent of convicted killers admitting to drinking before or during their acts back in the late 1800s. The gunfights of this period likely involved alcohol in some way.

By 1881, the population had reached six thousand. At the height of the town's growth, in 1885, the community was nearly ten thousand, making it the largest city in the territory. By 1884, the miners had harvested $25 million in silver. The greatest challenge they faced was getting access to water. Until 1881, they had to haul it in from somewhere else. Eventually, Huachuca Water Company built a pipeline that stretched twenty-three miles, transporting water from the Huachuca Mountains.

The rough part of town was situated along Allen Street. All around it, respectable people struggled to earn a living and establish civilization as they had done elsewhere in the West. Four churches catered to different

Tombstone mine shaft in 1940. *Library of Congress.*

denominations (Catholic, Episcopalian, Presbyterian and Methodist), and there were two newspapers (the *Nugget* and the *Epitaph*), schools, lodges and lending libraries. Schieffelin Hall, a large, two-story adobe building, provided a stage for plays, operas, revues and all the respectable stage shows. The Bird Cage on Allen Street provided a stage for the disreputable ones.

The town developed a split personality. On the one hand, decent, God-fearing folk were trying to make a fair life for their families; on the other, the flashy, commercial town was full of soiled doves and tinhorn gamblers who catered to the wants and desires of the miners and cowhands.

In the darkest corners of society lurked a criminal syndicate that even a presidential proclamation and the looming possibility of military rule could not bring to justice. There was also a fundamental conflict over resources and land: the traditional, southern-style "small government" agrarianism of the rural cowboys contrasted with northern-style industrial capitalism.

Research has indicated that the Wild West was not as violent as one would believe based on movies and books. Homicides were not frequent in small towns, farming areas or mining communities. However, murder rates for these places were still high compared to today and to other parts of the United States throughout the 1800s, except for certain southern states during the Civil War and Reconstruction eras. However, it is important to recognize several factors that contributed to this.

Police protection was scarce in many places for years. Aside from big cities, law enforcement mainly revolved around county sheriffs, roving judges and United States marshals. Unfortunately, there were not enough of these to sufficiently cover the ground, leading to many mysterious disappearances and homicides going unsolved and unaddressed due to insufficient legal protection.

Lynchings were tragically typical in many areas. It was acceptable to take the law into one's own hands and dole out punishment to those accused of wrongdoing. All too often, the wrong person was killed. Even worse, minorities and some White people were unlawfully murdered with impunity, primarily to preserve White domination after the Civil War.

Domestic violence and other forms of child abuse weren't legally prohibited in much of the Old West. A man who abused his wife, children or even his stepchildren (even if it resulted in death) would be imprisoned or hanged, but the law rarely intervened in an abusive home situation otherwise. Women and children received unfair treatment, and few steps were taken to prevent it. However, the Temperance movement attempted to use this issue as a platform, garnering followers by calling for its prohibition.

Commercial buildings on Allen Street were almost in ruins in 1937. *Library of Congress.*

In many areas of the western frontier, there were large numbers of men without female companions. Additionally, certain establishments, such as the military, jails and mining camps, were known to be volatile due to boredom and sexual frustration among the participants. Logging camps, mining settlements and work camps were also hazardous spots, with many altercations resulting from even minor disagreements.

Mental health resources were also severely lacking. In larger cities, a plethora of mental health professionals were available, as well as pharmaceuticals to help manage issues. But out in the Old West, it was a totally different story. Those with mental problems had to rely on self-control, prayer or punishment to deal with their struggles. The "asylum" was only for the worst cases, and no one else received treatment. This made many parts of the Old West extra hazardous.

Despite the dangers in the Old West, many people still chose to travel and settle there. Contained within these pages are the stories of murder and mayhem that occurred in Tombstone, Arizona.

ONE OF THE BLOODIEST INTERSECTIONS IN AMERICAN HISTORY

In Tombstone, the crossroads of Fifth and Allen became known as one of the bloodiest intersections in American history. The harsh and unforgiving atmosphere of the town was often fueled by the arguments between two rival groups of gamblers who frequented the saloons in this part of Tombstone—the Slopers and the Easterners. They'd often clash across the various gambling tables that filled the bars at this notorious crossroads.

The people known as Slopers had grown up around the California goldfields or in the dangerous Barbary Coast district of San Francisco. These men would often head to the Comstock region in Nevada, betting against the hardened miners there. On the other side were Easterners—they came from east of the Pacific Slope. They had experience dealing faro in places like Dodge City, Kansas City, Denver and St. Louis.

The violent exchanges between these two groups eventually became known as the Tombstone Gamblers' War and were fought primarily over the faro tables. Average dealers at these tables were paid six to ten dollars nightly for their services, potentially making even more if they also took a percentage of the winnings. Miners made only around three dollars daily, and cowboys were lucky if they earned thirty dollars monthly.

This struggle between saloon men, professional gamblers and tough guys was fierce as they vied for a bigger piece of the valuable gambling money. Gambling was a highly lucrative business in most mining towns. Hence, those who could remain calm and rob cowboys, miners and other professionals at their games had the potential to earn a hefty profit.

Above: The corner of Fifth and Allen Streets. The rebuilt Oriental saloon is to the left. Virgil Earp was shot here as he left the saloon. *Wikimedia Commons.*

Left: Doc Holliday as he appeared in the early 1880s. *Library of Congress.*

J.H.(Doc.) Holliday, as he appeared in the early eighties.

ONE OF THE BLOODIEST INTERSECTIONS IN AMERICAN HISTORY

Johnny Tyler, a professional gambler, had heard of the potential wealth to be earned in Tombstone and made the journey there to try his luck. His timing could not have been more perfect, as he arrived right when the Oriental Saloon opened, igniting ongoing rivalries between gamblers trying to stake their claim to the faro profits available.

According to the *Arizona Star* paper, on August 27, 1880, J.E. Tyler of Tombstone appeared at the Palace Hotel one day before the opening of the San Augustin festival, which attracted gamblers from all over the globe. John Shanssey, Wyatt Earp's buddy and a former saloon owner in Fort Griffin, had just arrived by train from San Francisco ten days prior. Additionally, John Behan, an official with a penchant for gambling and always seeking higher office, checked into the Palace with his son on September 12.

It is almost certain that Doc Holliday also stopped in Tombstone on September 27. Given the popular nature of the festival, it would have been the perfect time for him to make a pit stop if he was traveling south from Prescott. With so many people in attendance, one newspaper noted, "It is hardly possible to make a step in the gambling room in which there seems to be an attraction to all classes of society."

If Doc needed further enticement to visit Tucson, both Virgil and Wyatt Earp rode up from Tombstone, Virgil to visit his parents in California and Wyatt as a deputy sheriff bringing a criminal to court. It's safe to assume they'd each have made a few visits to the gambling dens before departing.

The festival concluded on September 16, and Tyler returned to Tombstone by the twenty-third. This was recorded in the *Epitaph* on the twenty-fourth.

> *An altercation occurred at Vogan & Flynn's saloon* [where Jim Earp tended bar] *yesterday between Tony Kraker and Johnny Tyler, two well-known sporting men during which a weapon, or weapons, were drawn. Friends interfered, and further hostilities were prevented.*

Kraker was a close friend of the Earps, so much so that they even entrusted him with a large sum of money—$1,000, to be exact—to bring to them on the day of the gunfight with Curly Bill Brocious at Iron Springs in 1882.

Not too long after the events at Vogan & Flynn's, a brawl broke out in the Oriental Saloon, a more noticeable establishment due to its luxury and success. On October 12, 1880, the *Daily Epitaph* published an article about what happened:

About 12:30 on Sunday night [October 10], *a shooting affray took place at the Oriental saloon…between M.E. Joyce, one of the proprietors, and a man named Doc Holliday. During the early evening, Holliday had an altercation with Johnny Tyler, which boded a shooting scrape. Shortly before the shooting referred to occurred, Holliday and Joyce came into the Oriental. Joyce went to Tyler and told him to leave the saloon as he didn't want trouble. Tyler complied, and Joyce made the same request to Holliday. Holliday demurred, and Joyce and he got into an altercation.*

Holliday refused to leave the saloon, and Joyce, in a fit of rage, threw him out. Although city marshal Fred White had disarmed him, Holliday returned shortly after procuring another pistol. The proprietor and Holliday exchanged shots before Joyce, a huge man, pounced on Holliday and furiously beat him up. One of Holliday's shots struck Joyce in the hand, so severely wounding it that amputation was considered. At the same time, another went through the foot of William Crownover Parker, Joyce's nineteen-year-old partner.

At the October 12 hearing on Holliday's attempted murder charge, Joyce, John Behan, Harry Woods and Fuller were the witnesses called to testify. These people were certainly not friends of either the Earps or those who supported them.

Lou Rickabaugh, Bill Harris and Dick Clark, owners of the prosperous concession at the Oriental, ultimately sided with the Easterners, even though Rickabaugh and Clark had initially moved to Tombstone from San Francisco. The connections in this fight for dominance were complex. On October 20, the *Daily Epitaph* mentioned that John Tyler was running a game of faro at Danner & Owens Hall, which happened to be located directly across the street from the Oriental. The *Daily Nugget*, on October 22, identified the proprietors of these faro tables as Charlie Smith and Robert J. Winders. These two were undoubtedly in a rivalry with Rickabaugh and some other people. Still, Smith and Winders were also good friends to the Earps and Holliday. James Earp once worked as a bartender for Winders in Fort Worth during the late 1870s, and the Earp brothers even became partners with Winder on some mining projects.

Rickabaugh's business partner, Bill Harris, was a veteran of the saloons of Dodge City, and he was well aware of the activities of Wyatt Earp and Doc Holliday. In fact, it may have been Harris who summoned Holliday to Tombstone in September 1880 to work as an enforcer to keep Tyler and his cohorts from stirring up trouble. This is even more likely given

Approaching the intersection of Fifth and Allen Streets in 1937. The rebuilt Oriental Saloon was a drugstore during this time. *Library of Congress.*

that Luke Short, another gambler skilled at handling firearms, arrived in Tombstone around the same time as Holliday, during the late fall or early winter of 1880.

Soon afterward, the showdown happened. John Tyler made a daring move to take over the Oriental, pointing his six-shooter at Lou Rickabaugh while he was seated behind a substantial heap of chips. Wyatt Earp acted quickly and grabbed hold of Tyler's ear, tossing him out of the saloon onto the street. Doc Holliday stayed inside, pointing his Colt revolver at Tyler's companions, keeping them in their places behind the bar. The meeting between Earp and Tyler likely happened in the middle of February 1881, and only a short time later, Charles Storms arrived in Tombstone from El Paso.

On February 25, 1881, Storms entered the Oriental Saloon. He tended to argue and had spent the whole night gambling, drinking low-quality whiskey and starting fights. On that morning, Luke Short was serving as the lookout, seated next to the dealer at a faro game in the Oriental. At thirty-two years of age, Short had already emerged victorious from numerous gunfights and was a seasoned gunman.

Charlie Storms was seated across from him. Storms was in his sixties and had seen plenty of fights. He had been at the shootout where Wild Bill Hickok was killed six years before, and it was said that he took away Wild Bill's gun as a keepsake when the dust settled.

An antique faro table that is still on display at the Bird Cage Theatre. *Library of Congress.*

Bat Masterson was friendly with both men. Despite the moral atmosphere in Tombstone of the 1880s, Masterson's relationship with Short and Storms was genuine. He desired to keep the peace between the two. When emotions ran high, he would attempt to mediate the situation.

The general idea is that Storms underestimated Short. Masterson declared afterward that Charlie must have thought Luke was the type he could beat up without consequences. But there's a timeless old saying among gunfighters: never underestimate your opponents. Storms would soon realize his mistake when he loudly accused Short of cheating. Masterson stepped in to prevent the situation from escalating and led Storms outside. He then attempted to soothe Short's nerves. Dr. George Goodfellow remained at a nearby table, sipping his drink throughout the incident.

Everyone was shocked when the intoxicated Storms reentered the saloon and forcefully moved toward Short. He shoved Masterson aside and clamped Short's right ear firmly in his left hand. Then he lunged for his gun.

Was it Short's superior skill that made him the victor? Maybe it was his comparative youth, or maybe his reflexes weren't impaired by alcohol like the other man's. In either case, Luke acted first. He pointed his Peacemaker pistol at Storm's chest and cocked the hammer back before releasing a

255-grain lead bullet directly into Storm's heart. He cycled his revolver and fired another bullet as Storms fell backward. The shot was so loud and forceful that it set Charlie's shirt ablaze.

The two shots sent Storms tumbling back nearly twelve feet and onto the ground. Even as he fell, he squeezed off two shots from his short single-action gun, yet neither found their mark. However, his body was lifeless when it hit the floor. Charlie Storms was beyond help. Short's shot pierced his heart and ricocheted off his spine. Although Dr. Goodfellow was not expecting it, the wound inflicted on Charlie Storms's chest was strangely bloodless. Once he sent the body off to the mortician and examined it, he realized why this had happened.

When Charlie Storms left home that morning, he tucked a small silk handkerchief into his left breast pocket. When Short's bullet hit the pocket, it was stopped by the delicate cloth, and remarkably, the silk was unharmed by the impact. The bullet didn't tear through the silk, as it would have other materials like cotton or wool; instead, the silk handkerchief encapsulated the penetrating bullet and remained intact in the wound. Dr. Goodfellow couldn't believe it. This discovery would eventually lead to the development of the bulletproof vest.

Marshal Ben Sippy took Luke Short into custody, accusing him of murder. However, thanks to the testimony of Bat Masterson, Short was let go after it became evident that this was an act of self-defense. Despite being a skilled gunman, Short died at thirty-nine from Bright's Disease, a complicated kind of kidney ailment that would have been a very unpleasant way to die back in the late 1800s.

Aside from the gambling feud, Fourth and Allen saw its fair share of violence. John Hicks was the first person to be laid to rest in Boothill Graveyard. John Hicks, born in August 1849, was an ordinary man until he became part of the history books in 1879. He studied science at Johns Hopkins University and then became a pharmacist. Drifting west, Hicks spent five years mining for gold in California before joining Professor Nathaniel Lupton from Vanderbilt University to explore Mexico in 1878.

After learning about the abundant silver lode in Tombstone, Hicks journeyed to the town in 1879 to stake his claim. Then his father arrived and helped him set up a mining company. Together, they bought mining equipment worth a small fortune. John's brother, Boyce, was also summoned to help with the claim out west.

In 1879, Tombstone was still more like a camp than a town, and the commercial establishments were housed in tents. The most popular tent saloon was Danner & Owens, which served whiskey for two bits and was where all the tough guys gathered. In this saloon, John Hicks became the first person from Tombstone to reside in Boothill Graveyard permanently. The event was first chronicled in the *Arizona Citizen*:

> *The town of Tombstone was thrown into a state of excitement by a shooting affray which occurred here last night at 11 o'clock. Seems that in the early evening of July 10th, 1879, a feud between Jeremiah McCormick and a man named Quinn was the catalyst for the events that would unfold later that evening when Quinn, liquored up, stopped in front of Danner & Owens and exclaimed that he could "whip any man in town."*

Apparently, McCormick interpreted the comment as an affront to him and responded by punching Quinn on the nose with such force that he fell to the floor. Quinn quickly bounced back up, and the men engaged in a physical altercation until Quinn conceded defeat.

Later that night, Quinn ran into his friend John Hicks and relayed the story of the day's events. The two then headed to Danner & Owens, where

The Dodge City Peace Commission, June 10, 1883. *Standing, from left*: William H. Harris (1845–1895), Luke Short (1854–1893), William "Bat" Masterson (1853–1921), William F. Petillon (1846–1917). *Seated, from left*: Charlie Bassett (1847–1896), Wyatt Earp (1848–1929), Michael Francis "Frank" McLean (1854–1902), Cornelius "Neil" Brown (1844–1926). *Wikimedia Commons.*

Hicks continued his dispute with McCormick. They traded insults until Hicks returned in fury to his tent, recounting what had gone down to his sibling.

John and Boyce headed back to Danner & Owens, armed with rifles and ready to fight. As they met McCormick and Jackson outside the building, heated words were exchanged before guns were drawn. Then six shots went off, five from McCormick and one from Jackson. John Hicks was killed instantly, and Boyce was severely wounded.

Deputy Sheriff Babcock arrested McCormick and Jackson, after which Fatty Smith removed John Hicks's body to his saloon. Once there, a coroner's inquest began. The verdict was that John Hicks "came to his death by a pistol ball shot by the hand of an unknown person." John's brother, Boyce, survived the gunshot but not without suffering from blindness for the rest of his life.

Another odd occurrence happened when a person named Frank Leslie showed up in Tombstone in July 1880, wearing the buckskin clothing of an outdoorsman. He swapped out his frontier duds for more sophisticated attire like those seen in San Francisco. However, he kept one item: a fringed buckskin vest. After that, folks knew him as "Buckskin Frank" Leslie. Later, he and William H. Knapp opened a saloon next door to the Cosmopolitan Hotel on Allen Street.

Leslie had taken a shine to Mary Jane "May" Killeen, a chambermaid at the Cosmopolitan Hotel. He attended her nuptials to Mike Killeen on April 13, 1880, in Tombstone, and his name was listed as one of the witnesses on the marriage document. Little did Leslie know that Mike had already become jealous of their relationship.

On the night of June 22, 1880, Leslie embraced May on the Cosmopolitan Hotel's front porch as her husband approached. Their friend George M. Perine noticed and warned them, but it was too late. Killeen fired his gun twice, grazing Leslie's scalp in the process and stunning him—so much so that Killeen was able to beat Leslie with his revolver before he himself was shot and mortally wounded by an unknown assailant. Before he passed away five days later, Killeen told E.T. Packwood that Perine had pulled the trigger. Leslie and Perine were both charged with murder, though Leslie argued he had done it in self-defense and Perine had not actually fired his weapon. The court accepted his explanation and dismissed the charges against both men.

It had only been eight days since Mary Killeen's husband passed away. Yet she still decided to marry Leslie. Thirteen-year-old Louisa E. Bilicke was honored to serve as the bride's maid of honor for a second time within

The Crystal Palace Saloon, Allen and Fifth Streets, in 1937. *Library of Congress.*

eighty-four days. The *Tombstone Epitaph* gave an account of the wedding in their newspaper.

> *July 6th, 1880, Wedding—Last evening, at 8 o'clock, Mr. N.F. Leslie was united in holy bonds of matrimony to Mrs. Mary Killeen (née Evans) by Judge Reilly. The wedding was a quiet one, only a few intimate friends of the parties being present. Miss Louisa Bilicke attended the bride, Col. C.F. Hines supporting Mr. Leslie. There were present during the ceremony, which took place in the parlor of the Cosmopolitan Hotel, Mr. and Mrs. Bilicke, Col. H.B. Jones and wife, Mr. C.E. Hudson and daughter, Miss French, Col. Hafford, Mr. E. Nichols, Mr. J.A. Whitcher, Mr. Maxon, Mr. J.A. Burres, Mr. Geo. E. Whitcher, F.E. Burke, Esq., and Mr. Fred Billings. At the conclusion of the ceremony, the bridal party and friends repaired to the dining room of the hotel, where a bounteous repast awaited them. The* Epitaph *congratulates Mr. Leslie, un chevalier sans peur et sans reproche,* [a knight without fear and beyond reproach] *and his most estimable wife upon this happy event and earnestly wishes them a pleasant voyage over life's troubled ocean.*

On May 26, 1882, Tombstone was engulfed in a massive fire that destroyed Knapp & Leslie's Cosmopolitan Saloon. The partners opted not to rebuild, and Leslie found employment at the Oriental Saloon, one of the few structures still standing.

On November 14, 1882, Leslie was working behind the bar at the Oriental. Billy Claiborne sauntered in and used insulting and abusive language fueled by his drunkenness. Leslie repeatedly told Claiborne to leave, but Claiborne persisted with foul language. So Leslie took matters into his own hands, grabbing Claiborne by his coat collar and escorting him out. Leslie later testified, "He used very hard language, and as he started away from me, shook a finger at me and said, 'That's all right, Leslie, I'll get even on you.'"

Only moments later, two men warned Leslie that a man was outside, ready to take aim. When Leslie looked outside, he saw a rifle barrel peeking out from behind a fruit stand. He attempted to talk sense into Claiborne, yet his pleas were disregarded. Claiborne pointed his rifle at

Inside the Crystal Palace in 1937. *Library of Congress.*

him and fired. Leslie, in response, shot back, striking Claiborne in the chest. "I saw him double up and had my pistol cocked and aimed at him again. I advanced upon him but did not shoot when he said, 'Don't shoot again. I am killed.'" The coroner's inquest determined that Leslie had acted in self-defense when shooting Claiborne, which "in the opinion of the jury, was justifiable."

Milton E. Joyce and Leslie decided to construct a ranch near Arizona's Swisshelm Mountains at the close of 1882, called the Magnolia Ranch. It was nineteen miles away from Tombstone in a very isolated area of southeastern Arizona. Milt sold his part of the enterprise to Leslie in 1885.

One year after their marriage, Mary Jane "May" Leslie filed for divorce, claiming that her husband had an affair with "Miss Birdie Woods" between July 4 and 6, 1886. She also claimed that Leslie physically abused her on March 9, 1887. On granting the request for a divorce on June 3, 1887, Judge William H. Barnes ordered Leslie to fork over $650 in cash and convey title to one-fourth of the Magnolia Ranch—complete with 13 horses and 150 cattle—as well as cover all legal fees associated with the case.

After his divorce, Mollie Edwards assumed the role of Leslie's "wife" at his ranch. But Leslie returned to the ranch on July 10, 1889, after drinking alcohol. He encountered Mollie Edwards seated and having a conversation with James Neil. The *Tombstone Daily Epitaph* later reported on this event.

> *Neil said that when Leslie returned, he came into the room where Neil and the woman were talking and without warning said: "I'll settle this!" and fired at the woman who fell from the chair without uttering a sound. Leslie then turned and fired two shots at Neil, the first taking effect in his left breast, near the nipple, and the other hitting him in the arm. He was unarmed and got out of the way as soon as possible.*

On July 12, 1889, Neil was brought to Tombstone, severely injured. His condition was treated by Dr. George E. Goodfellow. Leslie was apprehended that day, promptly jailed and had a two-day preliminary hearing, during which he was kept without bail until his trial in Tucson. The coroner's jury reported its verdict on the fourth day after Edwards's death.

> *After inspecting the body of the deceased and hearing the testimony, we find that the person killed was formerly known as Mollie Edwards; that at the time of her death, Frank Leslie claimed her as his wife; that on Wednesday, the 10th day of July 1889, at a place in Cochise County*

A drawing of the interior of the Alhambra Saloon. *Wikimedia Commons.*

known as "Leslie's Ranch," she came to her death by being shot with a pistol and by criminal means; and that she was, on the day aforesaid, shot and killed by Frank Leslie.

Leslie pleaded guilty to murder in the first degree on January 6, 1890. The *Sacramento Daily Record-Union* reported on the story.

It is expected he will receive a life sentence at Yuma. Leslie was noted for his bravery during the Custer massacre when he was employed as a scout and rendered valuable services to the Government under Crook and Miles in this section during the campaign of Geronimo and his band of cutthroats. He was a partner of the late M.E. Joyce of the Baldwin Hotel in a large cattle ranch in this country.

On January 9, 1890, Leslie was sent away to Yuma Territorial Prison for life after being sentenced by Sheriff John Slaughter. He became known there as inmate number 632. It had been less than three months since Leslie had

The bank building on the corner of Third and Allen Streets in 1937. *Library of Congress.*

been imprisoned when he attempted to break out with five other inmates. He was sent to solitary confinement for his participation in the escape plan. On release from isolation, Leslie became a model prisoner and worked as a pharmacist at the prison hospital. In late 1893, W.H. Cameron of the *San Francisco Chronicle* interviewed him.

> *His lot in prison is not a hard one. He does not wear the prison garb and is not confined to a cell at night. His conduct is perfect. Superintendent [Thomas] Gates said that he was the best-behaved prisoner and the most useful in the penitentiary. In case of sickness, the physician is called in and diagnoses the case while Leslie fills the prescription and administers the medicine. His drug store is the acme of neatness.*

An article in the *San Francisco Chronicle* inspired a thirty-six-year-old divorcée named Belle Stowell to write a letter to Leslie. The *Tombstone Prospector* newspaper reported that Governor Benjamin J. Franklin of Arizona was considering pardoning Leslie. Eventually, on November 17, 1896, the governor granted him a full and unconditional pardon. Soon after, Leslie left Arizona for Los Angeles.

One of the most notorious acts of violence at Fourth and Allen occurred late in the evening on December 28, 1881. Virgil Earp, who had been residing at the Cosmopolitan Hotel, where he was staying for protection from threats, was walking from the Oriental Saloon when he was ambushed.

Covered board sidewalk on Fifth Street, just north of Allen Street, in May 1940. Jack Crabtree's Livery Stable and the San Jose Lodging House can be seen on the left. *Library of Congress.*

The assailants were never officially identified, but it is presumed they were family or allies of the men who died in the O.K. Corral shootout. While Ike Clanton's hat was found near the scene of the crime, he did have an alibi backed up by his friends. Other suspects included Phin Clanton and Pony Diehl. The *Springfield Daily Republican* of December 30, 1881, included a report: "A United States Marshall Shot." The report reads:

> *Deputy Marshal Earp was fired on while crossing Fifth Street in Tombstone, Ariz., Wednesday night by three men, armed with shotguns, who escaped in the darkness. Nineteen shots hit Earp....The assault is undoubtedly the outgrowth of a recent fight with cowboys in which Earp was engaged. The gang have since threatened the lives of Earp and his supporters, and the citizens are greatly excited.*

The assailants fired from the second story of a building across Allen Street, which was empty due to construction. Witnesses to the event later estimated that five or six rounds from a shotgun were fired. Around twenty pellets were spread throughout the Crystal Palace Saloon and Eagle Brewery in the area near where Virgil was standing when it happened. Shards of glass flew everywhere as windows were broken by the shots, but luckily, none of the bystanders were hit. The same amount of buckshot pellets slammed into Virgil, though he did not collapse, and the shots were mainly concentrated on his back and left arm. He ended up with a permanently damaged arm due to the surgery that removed five and a half inches of his broken humerus during treatment for his injuries.

As his physicians assessed his wounds, Virgil, in great pain, could still communicate a few words to his spouse: "Never mind, I've got one arm left to hug you with."

A historical photograph of Virgil Earp, the chief of police in Tombstone. *Wikimedia Commons.*

When news of Virgil's serious injuries reached him, Crawley P. Dake, the U.S. marshal for that area, assumed the attack had been fatal, and he gave Wyatt the role of deputy U.S. marshal in place of his brother.

Today, visitors meander through the intersection of Fifth and Allen, unaware of the destruction and loss of life that took place here in the past.

CHAPTER 2

TILL DEATH DO US PART

The town of Tombstone is a living, breathing memorial to love found and lost. Among these deserts are sad tales of jilted lovers and romances gone astray.

One of the most notable tales was recorded in the *Tombstone Epitaph* on Saturday, April 14, 1888. Entitled "A Bloody Tragedy," it relates the sad story of George Daves and Pietra Edmunds.

> *Our usually quiet city was thrown into the most intense excitement yesterday by a tragedy such as never before occurred here. About 2 o'clock in the afternoon, passers-by on Third Street, near Safford, observed a young man, George Daves by name, running after a young woman named Pietra Edmunds and firing at her with a six-shooter. He fired three shots, one of which took effect in the woman's shoulder, after which he placed the pistol to his temple, pulled the trigger, and the ball went through his brain, causing death in a few minutes.*
>
> *The cause of the tragedy was jealousy. Young Daves had been paying attention to Miss Edmunds, but the day before yesterday, it is stated that they quarreled, and this so preyed upon the young man's mind that his reason, never very strong, became dethroned. He had recently come from Casa Grande, near which place he is said to have some valuable mining claims, and found on his return that he had been replaced in the affections of the young lady.*

At the time of the shooting, Miss Edmunds was passing by the residence of the unfortunate young man's father, corner of Third and Safford, in company with Fred Stone when young Daves ran out of the house, revolver in hand, and pointed it at Stone. The young woman screamed and ran across the street towards her own home. This diverted Daves' attention from Stone, who ran up town after an officer. In the meantime, Daves pursued his former sweetheart to her very door, firing as they ran. Only one bullet took serious effect. It entered the back of the young lady near the shoulder blade, passed through the right lung and out of the breast. At 9 o'clock this morning (Saturday), she was resting easily, and there are strong hopes of her recovery.

George Daves was 21 years old and was always considered a quiet, honest, industrious boy. His parents are highly respectable people and have the most sincere sympathy of the people of this community. The bereaved mother is now in California. The fond father takes the loss of his oldest son very hard.

The young woman who was the cause of all the trouble (perhaps innocently) is about 17 years old and is the daughter of the late Eugene Edmunds (known as "Stockton"), her mother being a Mexican and also dead. She is quite pretty and is worth some property.

An inquest will be held on the body of Daves at 2 o'clock this afternoon at Ritter's undertaking rooms, and the funeral will take place at 2 o'clock tomorrow (Sunday) from the same place.

An inquest was held by the Justice of the Peace for Township One, Cochise County, M.D. Shearer. Perhaps because of the shocking nature of the crime, anyone remotely involved was interviewed, and some of their testimony is presented here.

Dr. G.E. Goodfellow testified as to the fatal wound in George's head.

I found he was killed with a bullet wound to the head. The bullet entered in the right cheek and came out of the top of the head.

In an interview, Fred Dodge, Wells Fargo Express man and a friend of Wyatt Earp, said:

When I got there, I found Daves lying just outside of the gate, a pistol in his hand, bleeding from some wounds on the head. I took the pistol out of his hand and examined it, and went on into the house. In the second room, I found a young girl there bleeding, and she said she was shot. I helped take

The front of St. Paul's Episcopal Church, located at the intersection of Safford and Third Streets. George Daves lived in a house across the street. Built in 1882, the church is listed in the National Register of Historic Places. *Library of Congress.*

her in the bedroom and put her on the bed, and went after a doctor. I got Dr. Goodfellow to attend her and went back in there with him. Mr. James came then, and I left the house in his charge and came away. That is all I know about it.

From an interview with C.F. Hines, forty-two, a miner:

I and Mr. Cook was coming up Third St. when I saw the shooting as we were coming up the street by Edmunds' house. I saw the girl standing inside the gate. The next I heard shots going off. I looked around on the opposite side of the street, near Daves' house. The girl was running diagonally across the street towards her own house. This young man, Daves, was chasing her with a six-shooter in his hand. He shot at her three times while running across the street. I could not tell whether she was hit or not. She ran into the house. He stopped right on the outside of the gate, pulled up the six-shooter right against his head, and pulled it off. As he was standing up, he pulled it this way (illustrating) and held it about six inches from his head. When it went off, his head and the whole of his body went up in the air, just like that (illustrating), and he fell.

I came up the street and notified all the people I saw. I did not see any policeman on the street at that time. I went back there in about 15 minutes

31

and saw Mr. Oaks and Mr. Bartholemew, also. The body of a man was where he fell, and the blood all around on the ground. That is all I have to say about it.

The next woeful tale occurred on February 23, 1883, when May Woodman shot and killed William Kinsman. The tragedy shook up the town, which had grown used to gunfights and violent deaths. Even today, many are still fascinated by the story of Kinsman's death and the subsequent trial.

William Kinsman, nicknamed Billy, entered the world in Gwennap, England, in 1854. He was the eldest son of John and Catherine Kinsman, who had tied the knot nearly four years prior. John worked as a miner, and his son inevitably followed in his footsteps as soon as he was old enough.

It was around 1879 that Billy chose to emigrate to the United States. His parents bravely decided to follow him, and their three daughters, Catherine, Mary Ann and Elizabeth, came along too. Initially, Billy got employment in a mine near Virginia City in Nevada. In 1880, he moved farther south with John and Catherine to Tombstone, Arizona. They acquired a home at the corner of Toughnut Street and Seventh Street.

It is assumed that Billy and his father worked in one of the Tombstone mines that made up the hillside landscape of the town. All was going well until 1883, when a fatal gunshot killed Billy outside the Oriental Saloon.

The newspapers often referred to Billy Kinsman as a "sporting man," which is just a euphemism for somebody who frequents saloons and gambling dens. Tombstone had plenty of such places, so finding what he was looking for was easy. During the last part of his life, he appeared to be having an affair with a woman named Mary Woodman.

It was 1855 when Mary McIntyre, daughter of Henry and Ellen McIntyre, first came into the world. In 1880, Mary and her husband, Louis Woodman, were already separated. The following year, Louis placed a notice in the *Tombstone Epitaph* newspaper.

To whom it may concern. I hereby warn all persons against giving my wife, Mary Woodman, any credit on my account, as I will not be responsible for any debts contracted by her. She having left my bed and board without just cause or provocation, signed Louis C Woodman.

It appears Lewis sensed something wrong about his wife, who used the names Mary and May interchangeably. News articles published after the shooting assert that Billy and May had a close relationship at this time, potentially even living together. Still, the leading cause of the following catastrophe occurred in December 1882.

An announcement was posted in the *Tombstone Epitaph* on December 22, declaring that Billy Kinsman had gotten engaged to "May." However, this was merely a trick by some of his friends—they had simply changed her name, but it was clear to most people in the small town that it was a joke. To make matters worse, the *Epitaph* printed a response at Billy's request three days later.

> *Some unprincipled person came into this office a few days ago and requested us to publish the announcement of a marriage between William Kinsman and May Holzerman, which we did. It has since been discovered that no such occurrence ever took place. The alleged bridegroom denounces the statement as an unmitigated falsehood.*

If the May in question was actually "Woodman," not "Holzerman," it could have sparked anger toward her lover. Not only had Kinsman's acquaintances embarrassed her with their incorrect announcement, but when Billy refuted it, she also appeared to be a scorned lover. Having been publicly rejected by Billy and ridiculed in front of his friends, May was undoubtedly humiliated. No one knows how long she had plotted her revenge, but it's evident that this cruel prank caused the events of a few weeks later.

A little after ten o'clock, Alphanzo Ayala, a laborer, spotted May Woodman and Billy Kinsman talking outside the Oriental Saloon. He couldn't make out what they were saying, but he noticed May had her hand tucked under her cloak. Then, all of a sudden, he saw her pull out a gun and shoot Kinsman in the chest.

Thomas Keefe, a carpenter just nearby, testified to hearing a gunshot and then seeing Kinsman clutch his chest. As Keefe approached, he saw May Woodman grasping a nickel-plated "Bulldog" firearm in her right hand. He seized May and asked her what she was doing. She responded harshly with: "None of your damned business."

May was about to shoot at Kinsman again, but Keefe grabbed her arm and pushed it down, causing the bullet to ricochet off the wooden sidewalk. Just then, police officer James Coyle appeared and grabbed May's arms. The two men reported she was quiet and composed.

A local physician, H.M Matthews, testified in court that he noticed two gunshots and went to investigate. When he arrived at the scene, he found Kinsman lying on the ground with an injury. The bullet had pierced the left side of Kinsman's chest near his nipple, exiting near his right shoulder blade.

Two hours later, Kinsman passed away due to what the doctor suspected was internal bleeding.

May was detained in prison until her court date, which saw a panel of nine men, Pat Holland, the coroner and, eventually, Judge Pinney all listening to testimony from witnesses associated with the case.

Apart from the events of that day, more facts came to light during the trial, and not all of them were flattering to Billy. Speaking in defense of May, Dr. George Goodfellow argued that she was with child at the time of her apprehension. He also noted that while she was behind bars, she had attempted suicide and likely lost the baby due to the maltreatment she endured.

Another doctor, Daniel McSwegan, had been called to the Woodman house by May and Billy before the horrible incident. The couple asked him about the paternity of May's yet-to-be-born baby. May seemed uncertain about whether Billy had fathered her child as he only had one testicle, which made her think he was infertile. It goes without saying that this pointed to other potential fathers for her baby. McSwegan also testified that the couple had requested a potion for May to drink to terminate the pregnancy. He declared he refused to furnish it.

By the start of May 1883, all the evidence had been presented to the jury. The judge, Daniel Pinney, then proceeded to give his summation.

> *Although the jury may believe from the evidence that the deceased and the defendant lived together in open adultery and although the jury may further believe from the evidence that the deceased got the defendant in the family way and that deceased tried to have the defendant take medicine for the purpose of procuring an abortion still all this would not justify the defendant in taking the life of the deceased.*

It took the jury only thirty minutes to decide on a verdict. Even though May had been accused of murder, they found her guilty of manslaughter and gave her a five-year sentence at Yuma Prison. As soon as the sentence was announced, May shouted, "May God curse you forever."

The newspaper articles and trial documents left many questions unanswered. Was it true that May was pregnant with Billy's child? Did he feel as though he was being forced into marriage? Who proposed they get rid of the baby? How did May believe she could marry Billy when she still had a husband?

May was only the second woman to be incarcerated in Yuma, and there's reason to believe she was sexually abused by prison staff. Her mother commenced a campaign for her release, gathering over two hundred signatures from Tombstone citizens, including many of the jurors. In the summer of 1883, after she'd served just three months of her sentence, H.M. Van Arman, acting governor of Arizona, gave May a conditional pardon.

During her trial, May had proclaimed she was mentally unstable and urged the judge to "contact San Francisco for proof" of her state. To safeguard his people, Van Arman determined that May should be freed as long as she never returned to Arizona.

The Wild West was a breeding ground for young men with few women to fulfill their romantic desires. Consequently, the towns adopted nicknames for those who filled this intimate void, such as *good-time girls*, *shady ladies*, *soiled doves* and *ladies of the night*. A woman of a certain standing in society might call herself a *courtesan*. Other less-than-respectable women listed more creative titles on census reports, such as *ceiling expert* or *horizontally employed*.

This is the ill-fated romance of a gambler named Billy Milgreen and two Tombstone performers, Little Gertie the Gold Dollar and Margarita. All three lived in the famous Allen Street area of Tombstone.

The Bird Cage Theatre, Allen Street, near Sixth Street, in 1937. *Library of Congress.*

It is unclear where the Gold Dollar's moniker originated, though there's a possible connection to Milgreen. When Little Gertie, the petite blonde woman, began working as an entertainer at the Crystal Palace, she was given her new name. Nobody but Milgreen knew her actual name.

The backstory behind the nickname Gold Dollar is contested. Some say it was inspired by Little Gertie's golden hair, while others suggest a love affair with her cost a gold dollar. Regardless, this alias of hers fit right in with the other names of people in the town, like Lizzette the Flying Nymph and Crazy Horse Lil.

Gold Dollar was the belle of Tombstone. She was a popular shady lady known for her welcoming smile and fiery character, which were soon to be tested in a love triangle.

Things between Milgreen and Gold Dollar were all good until Margarita appeared on the scene. This tall, dark-haired beauty came to Tombstone for a job at the Bird Cage Theatre, performing onstage and off with customers. One night, she was attracted to Milgreen, who was in a relationship with Gold Dollar. Margarita figured it would be easy for her to seduce him away from his current partner, and if it came down to physical confrontation, she was confident she could take care of the petite blonde woman.

However, Gold Dollar couldn't help how she felt: she had fallen head over heels in love with Milgreen. Whenever she had a few minutes to spare at the Crystal Palace, she would find him and wrap her arms around him for an embrace and a kiss goodbye.

At the same time, Margarita was trying to win Milgreen over. She flirted with him shamelessly every time he stepped into the Bird Cage. However, Margarita didn't realize that Gold Dollar had patrons at the joint who kept her up to date on Margarita's daring attempts to snatch away her boyfriend.

One fateful night, Gold Dollar charged into the Bird Cage after being tipped off by her friend, and she quickly caught sight of Margarita sitting in Milgreen's lap. She burst through the entrance and shouted, "Get away from my man, you Mexican chippy! I warned you before! You need to stay away from my man this time, you Mexican chippy! I gave you fair warning." With that, Gold Dollar seized a bunch of Margarita's long dark hair and threw her onto the ground. The fiery Latina sprung back up with fists raised, ready to fight, but the more petite woman was no match for her. In desperation, Gold Dollar reached for the double-edged stiletto hidden in her garter belt and stabbed Margarita directly in the heart.

A doctor was summoned to the Bird Cage and, on witnessing Margarita lying on the ground in a pool of her own blood, immediately declared that

The theater was named for the bird cages that lined both sides of its interior. *Library of Congress.*

it was too late for help. He then walked over to the bar and ordered himself a shot of whiskey.

When Gold Dollar heard that the sheriff was approaching, she quickly exited the Bird Cage Theatre through the back door and disposed of the knife. As a result, no evidence was discovered linking her to the murder; thus, she was not charged for the crime. Not long after this incident, Gold Dollar vacated the town. Milgreen also left, but there is no proof that they came together or met up at any point afterward. Margarita's body was eventually laid to rest in Boothill Graveyard.

In 1982, a vintage stiletto was discovered in the back of the Bird Cage Theatre, and it is suspected to be the knife that Gold Dollar used to stab Margarita. It is now featured as an exhibit at the Bird Cage Theatre.

It's impossible to prove the truth of this story or definitively discount it as a tall tale. It has undoubtedly been told more than once, like the tale of the Lost Dutchman's Mine. Very few people know the true identity of Gold Dollar, for she—like many others in her trade—was careful to keep it a secret. Some retired by marrying, while others passed away due to addiction, substance abuse or illness; they are buried with no mark to distinguish them.

Paintings of circus scenes adorned the bird cages that lined the interior of the old theater and saloon. *Library of Congress.*

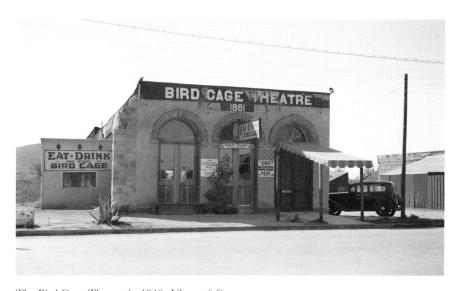

The Bird Cage Theatre in 1940. *Library of Congress.*

The passage of time has brought about a transformation in these formerly notorious bawdy houses, for they now serve as museums. Ladies from the local historical society come to give talks on the life and times of those bygone courtesans.

CHAPTER 3

GUNFIGHT AT THE O.K. CORRAL

March 1881 was a fateful month for the stagecoach traveling between Tombstone and Benson. Two passengers were killed in an ambush, but Pima County sheriff Bob Paul managed to keep the $26,000 Wells Fargo lockbox safe. Years later, in 1896, Wyatt Earp told the story in the *San Francisco Examiner*.

> *The moment the first shots were fired and Philpott fell, the horses plunged ahead so viciously that nothing could have stopped them. In missing the messenger and killing the driver, the robbers had defeated their own plans.*

Virgil, Wyatt and Morgan Earp, Johnny Behan, Bob Paul, Bat Masterson and Wells Fargo agent Marshall Williams banded together to pursue the perpetrators of a holdup. They followed their trail to a ranch near Benson, where they encountered Luther King, who confessed that he and his accomplices, Jim Crane, Harry Head and Billy Leonard, were behind the crime.

King later managed to break out of the Tombstone jail, and Wells Fargo offered rewards of $1,200 each for Crane, Head and Leonard. Despite gossip that the Earps and Doc Holliday were also involved in the robbery, there was no proof of this.

By June 1881, the three fugitives were still on the run. Wyatt formulated an idea that would work out for him in multiple ways. He attempted to bribe Ike Clanton, Joe Hill and Frank McLaury into luring their wanted counterparts into town. Once Wyatt apprehended them, he would give his

The robbery of the stagecoach traveling between Tombstone and Benson escalated the tensions between Wyatt Earp and Ike Clanton. *Library of Congress.*

loyal informants the $3,600 reward money. Plus, he knew it was an excellent opportunity for him to win the election for Cochise County sheriff, something much more valuable than just the reward payout.

The agreement between Ike Clanton and Wyatt Earp soon unraveled when it was discovered that Leonard and Head had already been slain by rustlers in New Mexico's Animas Valley. So Ike was now stuck with a quandary: if anyone heard he'd entered into an understanding with Wyatt to turn on his fellow desperadoes, regardless of how the agreement ended, his name, and possibly even his life, would be put in jeopardy.

As 1881 wore on, Ike Clanton's luck only got worse. In August, Old Man Clanton and four other men lost their lives in the Guadalupe Canyon Massacre at the hands of Mexican smugglers. The fact that Jim Crane, the sole surviving suspect from the Benson stagecoach incident, was among them made things even more bitter for Ike. The Clanton patriarch had always kept his kin under control through political connections and local influence. Still, with his passing, it was anyone's guess as to what would become of the family. Writes Jeff Guinn in *The Last Gunfight*:

> With Old Man Clanton in the grave, Ike was finally free to act however he pleased without worrying about how his father might respond afterward. It was now a matter of which foolish, potentially lethal thing Ike might do first.

For the following weeks, Ike accused Wyatt of revealing their negotiations to other people. He didn't appear to comprehend that Wyatt was not keen to make public their arrangement either. It wouldn't come across well to voters if he was known to conspire with cowboys, just as current sheriff Johnny Behan had.

It was common for a card game to last all night at the Occidental Saloon in Tombstone, Arizona. However, the card game that ended on October 26, 1881, before seven o'clock in the morning was a game none would forget. And it wasn't just the card players, the whole country wouldn't forget it, either. This is because four of the five participants later took part in the most famous gunfight in the history of the American West.

Wyatt Earp aged around thirty-nine, circa 1887. *Wikimedia Commons.*

The name of the fifth man at the table is lost to history. The players around the table that evening included Virgil Earp, the chief of police; Johnny Behan, the Cochise County sheriff; Ike Clanton, a rancher and rustler; and Ike's cowboy friend Tom McLaury, who also had questionable ties.

The early morning hours of the twenty-sixth saw Clanton's losses mounting and his frustration rising. He fixated on past run-ins with Doc Holliday and Wyatt Earp, brother of Virgil Earp, who was participating in the poker game. Once it came to light that Virgil was carrying a firearm while playing, Clanton was furious, believing this indicated a conspiracy between Virgil, Holliday and Wyatt Earp to kill him. Ike demanded that Virgil take a message to Holliday insisting he must fight, but Virgil refused, warning Clanton not to cause further trouble. This resulted in Ike's threatening reply that Virgil might have to fight sooner than he thought, adding the chief of police to the list of his targets since arriving in town with Tom McLaury the day before.

The feud between the Clantons and the Earps had been escalating for more than twelve months. Virgil Earp was now the most prominent lawman in town, and it was public knowledge that Wyatt wanted to be elected sheriff for Cochise County. In the Clanton gang's eyes, the Earps were a real danger to the Clantons' thieving habits.

In August, the Clanton gang's world was turned upside down following the death of their patriarch, Newman Haynes "Old Man" Clanton. As far as they could tell, Mexicans—possibly army irregulars—had killed him in retaliation for the gang's rustling expeditions south of the border. This tragedy threatened to end a profitable business and way of life.

Meanwhile, Ike was in a frenzy due to a pact he had cut with Wyatt Earp to sell out some of his acquaintances who had committed the Benson stage heist near Drew's Station on March 15, 1881. Ike was anxious that the whole plan was going awry and could sense that Wyatt had spilled details of the scheme to Doc Holliday.

Doc Holliday and Wyatt Earp had a long-standing friendship, but Doc was also close to Bill Leonard, one of the stage robbers Ike Clanton wanted to turn in. Holliday respected Wyatt's ambition to be sheriff, so while he wouldn't like it, he could live with Wyatt hunting down Leonard. But if he found out that Clanton had implicated his own acquaintances, then Doc would consider it a betrayal of his personal code of honor as a southern gentleman. Plus, if word got out of the plan, Ike would be in grave danger.

Unsure if Wyatt had told anyone else about the deal, Ike made a direct accusation against him in October. Wyatt denied it, but he knew his paranoid co-conspirator was suspicious. This prompted him to send his brother Morgan to Tucson to locate Holliday and bring him back to Tombstone. On the night of the twenty-fifth, they were all together at the Alhambra Saloon when Ike Clanton appeared.

When Ike stepped foot in town, he had to drop his Colt .45 revolver and Winchester rifle at the West End Corral to comply with Ordinance No. 9, which mandated visitors to disarm when they were in the city. Later, he ran into Wyatt Earp, Morgan Earp and Doc Holliday at the Alhambra, where he called them out for betraying him, though he was careful to divulge it as a rumor rather than a fact. The tension heightened quickly as Doc labeled him a "son of a bitch cowboy" and "damned liar" for supposedly threatening the Earps, then barked at him to draw his gun. Ike responded that he had no weapon, but Holliday's goading continued: "Go to fighting," Doc shouted, "if there is any grit in you." He kept his arm close to his chest, where Ike assumed he had a pistol.

The exchange between Ike and Doc quickly escalated into a heated argument that was audible from inside the neighboring Occidental Saloon. Virgil Earp marched outside to break it up, warning he'd arrest them all if they didn't quiet down. The bickering ceased, and each of them stomped off in opposite directions.

Meanwhile, Wyatt had gone to the Golden Eagle Brewery to inspect his faro concession. When he came back out, Clanton was waiting for him and challenged him to a fight. Although Wyatt refused the invitation and said there was no money in it, Ike persisted: "I will be ready for you in the morning."

As Wyatt walked into the Oriental, Ike continued his threats: "You must not think I won't come after you all in the morning." Despite this, Wyatt stayed firm and left without any indication of being intimidated.

Ike didn't want the night to end, so he headed to the Occidental, where he joined a poker game. When daybreak arrived, he was out and about again, and by eight o'clock that morning, he had stopped at the West End Corral to pick up his guns. He was supposed to leave town under orders of the law, but Clanton had other plans. He wanted to have a big day in Tombstone, and if he carried the weapons around, it was only for defensive reasons. He even said later, "I had those guns around my person for self-defense," as he was expecting to meet Doc Holliday on the street. Once Ike had acquired his guns, he went to the Oriental and encountered Ned Boyle, a bartender and friend of the Earps. It is rumored that Ike told Ned, "As soon as those damned Earps make their appearance on the street today, the ball will open. We are here to make a fight. We are looking for the sons-of-bitches."

Despite Ned's attempts to soothe Ike, Wyatt was eventually awakened and informed of Ike's belligerent comments. Although Wyatt was used to such tirades, he decided to check out the Oriental himself.

At nine o'clock in the morning, Officer A.G. "Andy" Bronk of Virgil's police force roused the chief from his slumber, warning: "There is likely to be hell! Ike Clanton has threatened to kill Holliday as soon as he gets up.… He's counting you fellows in, too." But Virgil just groaned and rolled over, attempting to go back to sleep. Later in the day, though, Virgil ventured down to the center of town to investigate what all the fuss was about.

At around ten o'clock in the morning, Ike Clanton was conversing with Joe Stump at Julius A. Kelly's Wine House. The barkeeper listened as he poured drinks for both men. Ike told him that he had been unarmed when he was insulted by Earp's group earlier that morning; however, now he declared that he was "heeled" and ready to "fight on sight." He had been ranting about the same thing all morning, but no one paid much attention to his words. Kelly assumed it was a more serious matter, so during the trial after the O.K. Corral battle, he testified that he had warned Ike against any fight since he believed the other party would not shy away from defending themselves if provoked.

Shortly after noon, Clanton stumbled, intoxicated, into Hafford's Corner Saloon, a popular hangout for the Earp brothers. He asked Colonel Roderick Hafford about the meeting between himself, the Earps and Holliday that was supposed to happen at noon. Hafford told him it was already past that hour, and there was no point in going. "There will be nothing of it," the saloon owner added, telling Ike that he should just go home.

Eventually, Clanton went to Camillus Fly's boardinghouse, where Doc Holliday was staying with "Big Nose" Kate. Doc was sleeping when Ike arrived, and Mollie Fly, the landlord's wife, warned Kate that Ike was lurking outside, armed to the teeth. Kate woke her common-law husband, and Doc replied: "If God lets me live long enough to get my clothes on, he shall see me."

John Clum, mayor of Tombstone and owner of the *Tombstone Epitaph*, stepped out for lunch just down the street from his office. As he walked out, he ran into Ike Clanton at Fourth and Fremont Streets. "Hello, Ike! Any new war?" Clum inquired jovially, not realizing the irony of his question. Fortunately for him, Clanton did not answer. A short while later, Clum encountered Sheriff Charlie Shibell. Just then, Virgil and Morgan Earp rounded the corner onto Fourth Street with their guns drawn, headed straight for Clanton, who had yet to spot them.

Virgil seized Ike's rifle from his left hand, and as Clanton moved to draw his gun, Virgil pulled out his own revolver and clobbered it against Ike's skull, making him kneel down. After this, Virgil asked Clanton if he had been looking for him. To this, Ike responded yes and boasted that he would have killed him had he caught sight of the sheriff a second sooner.

Virgil arrested Ike for breaking Ordinance No. 9 and took him to Judge Albert O. Wallace's courtroom. Unfortunately, Wallace was out conducting a marriage ceremony. Soon Wyatt arrived at the courtroom and Ike informed the Earp brothers that he would take revenge on all of them and said he'd fight if only he had a six-shooter. Morgan then offered Ike his own weapon, but before Ike could grab it, Deputy Sheriff Rezin J. Campbell pushed him back into his chair.

Fed up with Clanton's antics, Wyatt declared, "You damned dirty cow thief, you have been threatening our lives, and I know it. I will go anywhere on earth to fight with you, even over to San Simon among your crowd!"

Ike refused to give in, stating, "I will see you after I get through here. I only want four feet of ground to fight on."

As Wyatt walked away from the court, he crossed paths with Tom McLaury. McLaury, who was there to check on his buddy Ike, declared to Wyatt, "If you want to make a fight, I will make a fight with you anywhere."

At this provocation, an angry Wyatt used his left hand to slap McLaury's face and whipped out his six-shooter with his right. He taunted the cowboy into a fight, shouting at him to draw his gun and fight back. When McLaury hesitated, Wyatt backed up his words by smacking McLaury on the head with his gun before striding off toward Hafford's Corner Saloon.

Returning to the courthouse, Justice Wallace gave Ike Clanton a fine for carrying firearms in town. The charges came to twenty-five dollars plus court costs. Despite the setback, Clanton kept his defiant attitude, but he paid the penalty. Virgil then took custody of both weapons, Ike's rifle and his six-shooter, and transported them to the Grand Hotel for safekeeping until their owner could retrieve them.

Billy and Frank McLaury got wind of the brewing confrontation a while later and decided to come into Tombstone. When they arrived, the two joined Billy Allen at the Grand Hotel for a drink. Allen had heard about Wyatt's argument with Tom, and when Frank asked what it was about, Allen replied that he did not know. Frank determined it best to leave town to avoid more conflict and said they would not finish their drinks before hurrying away, leaving their glasses untouched on the bar. The Cochise County Cowboys ventured down Allen Street and connected with Billy Claiborne at Dexter's Livery Stable, where Ike had already arrived. Their plans to leave town were pushed back.

As the Cowboys approached Spangenberg's Gun Shop, Wyatt Earp was standing in front of Hafford's, smoking a cigar. Wyatt was intrigued when he noticed Ike and the others approaching the gun shop and followed them.

Frank's horse also seemed quite intrigued by the happenings inside the gun store. It took a few steps onto the boardwalk and nudged its nose through the door. Wyatt grasped the bit in one hand while Frank and Tom approached the door, Billy Clanton following close behind with his gun drawn.

"You all need to move this horse," Wyatt said calmly. Meanwhile, the Cowboys were loading up their gun belts with bullets. As far as Wyatt knew, they weren't doing anything illegal. After all, George Spangenberg denied them a gun when they asked for one. Still, the Cowboys' visit to the gun shop had Wyatt concerned.

Having no weapon, Ike Clanton hastened from the gun shop to the saloon. As he passed Virgil Earp on the street, he kept his mouth shut. Soon enough, Virgil got into a discussion with an out-of-town railroad worker, H.F. Sills, who reported that he had just come across four or five armed men at the O.K. Corral. One threatened to kill Virgil Earp, and the others responded by stating they "would kill the whole party of Earps."

It was around two thirty in the afternoon when Sheriff Behan tried to convince the Cowboys band to give up their arms, asking Frank McLaury to

The Earp brothers set out to disarm the Cowboys. Arizona reenactors Kyle Truhill, Bob Kenney and Zach Etter relive the "Town Too Tough to Die" days of the 1880s. *Library of Congress.*

do so for the sake of safety. However, Frank refused. He stated that as long as people in Tombstone were behaving this way, he would not surrender his guns. Then Behan proposed to take Frank and the rest of the Cowboys to his office, which was considered a secure place. The sheriff and Frank went to the area adjacent to Fly's boardinghouse, where Ike, Billy, Tom and the others were waiting. Behan thought they would all come with him, but it was too late.

Virgil Earp was determined to disarm the Cowboys and, with his brothers Wyatt and Morgan and Doc Holliday, was on his way to a fateful rendezvous. Someone noticed the Earp party outside of Bauer's meat market on Fremont Street and shouted, "They're here!"

John Behan hurried away from the Clanton gang to appeal to Virgil not to go down there, or he would be killed. "I have to, Johnny," Virgil replied. But Behan claimed he had already disarmed the Cowboys. With that knowledge, Virgil switched his cane, given to him earlier by Doc Holliday, from his left hand to his shooting hand, while Wyatt placed his gun in his coat pocket. They continued on down the street as Behan watched them go.

As the Earps and Holliday advanced on the area, they noticed some of the Cowboys were armed. "Throw up your hands," ordered Virgil Earp.

"I've come to disarm you." Virgil desperately tried to stop the situation, lifting his cane futilely.

As Virgil spoke, Frank McLaury made a motion to draw his revolver. Wyatt Earp pulled his revolver and shot him, the ball striking the right side of McLaury's abdomen. At the same time, Doc Holliday shot Tom McLaury in the right side using a short shotgun.

Once a few shots had been fired, Ike Clanton came running forward and grabbed Wyatt Earp's left arm. Noticing that Ike did not have a weapon in his hand, Wyatt told him, "The fight has commenced. Go to fighting or get away."

That day, Ike Clanton had a moment of clarity and chose to flee for his life. He ran to Fly's and then Allen Street before making a final dash onto Toughnut Street, leaving behind his two friends and brother to face a shower of bullets.

At the same time, Billy Clanton shot Morgan Earp in the shoulder blade; the bullet grazed his spine and exited out of the opposite shoulder. Morgan dropped to the ground but quickly got up, and as Frank McLaury crossed Freemont Street, Morgan and Doc Holliday fired at him simultaneously. Both bullets found their mark, one hitting him in the right temple and the other in his left breast; either could have been fatal.

Tom McLaury stepped out on the pavement and pointed his weapon at Holliday, exclaiming: "I've got you now!" To which Holliday responded with a smirk, "Blaze away! You're a daisy if you have!" The bullet from McLaury's gun flew through Holliday's pocket, skimming his skin.

While that was happening, Billy Clanton fired a shot that hit Virgil Earp in his right leg, passing through the calf and leaving him with a nasty wound. Morgan Earp shot Clanton in the right wrist and left breast in response.

Frank and Tom McLaury were fatally wounded in the thirty-second shooting spree. Billy Clanton, amazingly, lived for an hour after the fight despite his injuries. The *Nugget*'s editor and foreman carried him to a nearby house and did their best to make him comfortable. Clanton never let out a groan of complaint, and just before he died, he uttered, "Goodbye, boys; go away and let me die." By three o'clock the following day, the wounded had been taken home and were resting peacefully.

As soon as news of the shooting reached the Vizina and Tough Nut mines, their whistles blared loudly to summon all miners to the surface. The men arrived outfitted with guns, looking like a conquering horde storming through town. In a few minutes, all the more capable citizens were prepared to face any trouble that might come their way. They took steps to maintain

Top: The infamous gunfight lasted less than thirty seconds. *Library of Congress.*

Bottom: Though it's still debated who fired the first shot, most reports say Wyatt Earp fired first as Frank McLaury made a motion to draw his revolver. *Library of Congress.*

law and order, including putting ten guards around the jail and increasing the police presence around the jail for the night.

The deceased Cowboys were placed side by side in the morgue, concealed with a sheet. Little blood was visible on their clothing, and only on Billy Clanton's face could one make out any indication of suffering. The McLaury brothers' facial expressions were as tranquil in death as if they had peacefully passed, surrounded by their adoring relatives and friends.

Mannequins grace the site of the gunfight. They are positioned from a map drawn by Wyatt Earp. *Wikimedia Commons.*

Finn Clanton, a brother of Billy and Ike, arrived in town and sought protection from the sheriff. Afterward, he visited the morgue to see his brother's remains and then spent the night in jail with his deceased brother.

Numerous sources detailing the events leading up to the gunfight and the fight itself are at odds with one another. Newspapers during that time were not above partisanship, and much of their coverage was editorialized to reflect their publishers' interests. John Clum, who owned the *Tombstone Epitaph*, played a significant role in organizing the "Committee of Safety," also known as a vigilance committee, that met in Tombstone in late September 1881. That year, he was elected as the first mayor under the new city charter. Clum's newspaper took the side of local business owners and supported Deputy U.S. Marshal Virgil Earp. Meanwhile, Harry Woods was Behan's undersheriff and publisher of the other major newspaper, the *Daily Nugget*. He and his newspaper tended to be more sympathetic to Behan, the Cowboys (some of whom were part-time ranchers and landowners) and rural interests associated with ranchers.

Much of what is known about the event comes from the Spicer hearings, a series of court sessions that lasted for about a month. Reporters from

Other maps drawn by witnesses of the gunfight placed the Earp party with their backs to the building and the Cowboys standing across from them. Regardless, the fight spilled out into Fremont Street. *Wikimedia Commons.*

The "Grid Block" in Tombstone, Arizona, housing (*left to right*) the Old Hotel Nobles, the *Tombstone Epitaph* and the Mining Exchange Building. The Mining Exchange was where the Earps and Doc Holliday defended themselves against murder charges after the Gunfight at the O.K. Corral. At far right is Schieffelin Hall. *Library of Congress.*

Above: The old City Hall building on Fremont Street (seen here in 1937) was where the trial of the Earps occurred. Today it is a parking lot. *Library of Congress.*

Left: The wooden tombstone of Billie Clanton and the McLaury brothers in Boothill Graveyard in 1937. Note the vandalism done to the wooden marker. *Library of Congress.*

The office of the *Tombstone Epitaph* on Fifth Street in 1940. *Library of Congress.*

both papers jotted down the testimony in their notebooks during the court session and inquest, but only the reporter from the *Nugget* had the skill to take notes in shorthand. The reports created by the court recorder and the two newspapers varied greatly.

The Earps claimed the fight was justified, as the Cowboys had gone against local law and refused to give up their guns. The other side of the story was that the Cowboys willingly raised their hands and never resisted yet still were shot down in cold blood by the Earps. It was hard to tell who was being truthful then, and it remains somewhat of a mystery even now.

Though the *Epitaph* and the *Nugget* were typically at odds in how they portrayed incidents, both papers' reporting initially backed up the story provided by the lawmen. Woods, the publisher of the Cowboy-friendly *Nugget*, was away during the hearings, so Richard Rule, a very seasoned newsman, wrote about what transpired. The staff of the *Nugget* had a tight connection to Behan, yet Rule's narrative in the issue of the paper released one day after the shootout lined up with what the Earps reported. This contrasted intensely with what Behan and the Cowboys said when they took the stand.

Stories published in the *Nugget* after the gunfight aligned with Behan's and the Cowboys' accounts of events. The *Epitaph*, however, painted an entirely different picture that corroborated the lawmen's stories. Dr. George Goodfellow, who conducted autopsies on the dead Cowboys, testified to the court that Billy Clanton's wrist wound indicated his hands couldn't have been up in surrender or holding his coat open by its lapels, as witnesses who sided with the Cowboys claimed.

CHAPTER 4
TERRITORIAL VOTER FRAUD

T he dirt streets of Tombstone were known not only for their excessive violence but also for their political corruption. The town's police force was run by a man named Johnny Behan, backed up by his deputies and the Cowboy faction working both sides of the Mexican-American border. This strange alliance would eventually be nicknamed the Ten Percent Ring.

Back in 1881, the *Tombstone Epitaph* gave Johnny Behan and his cohorts this nickname for stealing almost one-tenth of local taxes collected from Tombstone, Arizona. Milt Joyce, who owned the Oriental Saloon and held the position of chairman of the Cochise County board of supervisors, was considered to be at the helm of this illegal activity.

The *Tombstone Epitaph* revealed accusations of corruption against Cochise County sheriff Johnny Behan. As part of his salary, he was given 10 percent of all collected taxes on prostitution, gambling, liquor and theater activities. This sparked rumors that Behan headed the Ten Percent Ring and had connections with the outlaw Cochise County Cowboys. Accomplices included Artemus Fay, owner of the first Tombstone newspaper, the *Tombstone Weekly Nugget*, and Harry Wood, a writer for the *Nugget* who was also an undersheriff to Behan.

Apart from tax embezzlement, the Ten Percent Ring also played a role in electoral bribery and assisting the cowboy vigilantes of Cochise County. Behan was so lax on crime that shortly after becoming sheriff, Virgil Earp was appointed Tombstone's city marshal and his brothers Wyatt and Morgan became special deputy policemen. Behan and the Earps were at odds, as

Behan backed the outlaw Clanton and McLaury families. After the famous gunfight at the O.K. Corral and the assassination of Morgan Earp, Behan did nothing to track down the assassins. Rather than search for Morgan's murderers, Behan issued warrants against U.S. Marshal Virgil Earp and Wyatt for killing the outlaws they believed to be responsible.

On January 31, 1882, Behan was apprehended and taken to court after it came to light that he had asked for payment on the same bill twice. Justice Stilwell decided to let him off due to a loophole in the law. His attempts at re-election as sheriff that November were unsuccessful, and he never held a role as an officer of the peace again. Later, he was assigned the title of warden of Yuma Territorial Prison and took on various other government positions until he died in 1912.

Milt Joyce left Tombstone in 1883, and he passed away six years later in San Francisco at the age of forty-two. Not long before that, in 1880, he had a confrontation with Doc Holliday at the Oriental Saloon. Before his death, Joyce owned both the Baldwin Billiard Parlor and the Café Royal in San Francisco.

Having served in the Union infantry for Pennsylvania, Harry M. Woods relocated to Nogales, Arizona, where he worked as a tax collector until his passing in 1896. Artemus Fay was a writer for the *Weekly Nugget*, which the paper offices burned down during the 1882 fire and never reopened. He then got a job at the Dos Cabezas Nugget Mine and tried his hand at publishing when he created the *GoNote* paper shortly after. However, the paper quickly ended its run. After his wife's demise, Fay moved to Flagstaff and launched another newspaper there.

In addition to robbing Tombstone of part of its tax money, the Ten Percent Ring was heavily involved in electoral bribery, which started in 1880.

In 1877, Wells Fargo appointed Robert Paul to Arizona, where he forged a friendship with Pima County deputy sheriff Wyatt Earp. Three years later, Paul, who had become a U.S. deputy marshal since then, decided to vie for the office of sheriff on the Republican ticket in Pima County. Election Day painted a pro-Paul picture; he was leading his Democratic opponent, Charlie Shibell, by a significant margin. Undeterred by the results so far, the Democrats kept saying, "Wait until the returns from San Simon get here," and the *Tucson Citizen* reported that "a few of our New Mexico neighbors came across the line to aid their Arizona brethren."

A year before his involvement in the legendary gunfight at the OK Corral, Joseph Isaac "Ike" Clanton served as an election inspector for the San Simon precinct alongside John Ringo and A.H. Thompson, two notorious

Another city hall was eventually built and also served as a fire station. This photo was taken in 1937. *Library of Congress.*

gunslingers. The votes were certified and sent to the Pima County Board of Supervisors by one individual who identified himself as "Henry Johnson." Even though only approximately ten to twelve individuals on the voter registry resided in San Simon, 103 Democratic votes in favor of Shibell were certified, but only a single Republican vote for Paul was cast.

On November 15, 1880, Charles A. Shibell was approved as sheriff by the Pima County Board of Supervisors. Four days later, Paul requested copies of the poll lists from San Simon, Solomonville, Turkey Creek and Benson to compare them against the Pima County voter registration lists. At the same time, Shibell asked for the poll lists from Tombstone, Willcox, Camp Grant and Pajarita, suggesting that Paul's supporters had committed voting fraud in those areas.

Two teams of lawyers faced each other in the courtroom, ready to battle it out in the election dispute. For Paul, attorneys Warner Earll, F.M. Smith, G.W. Spaulding, Alexander C. Campbell, James F. Robinson and John Haynes appeared as counsel. Meanwhile, Shibell had secured the services of James C. Perry, Benjamin Morgan, Lyttleton Price, Charles Silent, Benjamin Hereford and James A. Zabriskie to represent him.

On December 18, Paul's legal team fought the election results in a district court. They claimed that "Henry Johnson" was a false identity, and thus, all San Simon votes should be canceled. Since Paul was a deputy marshal of the United States, he could subpoena several men whose names were included on the San Simon voting list. In the end, Paul discovered that "Henry Johnson" was actually James Johnson.

Johnson argued that a voter who wasn't on the list was refused in the presence of Republican observer R.B. Kelly in an attempt to seem honest. He presumed three or four actual ballots were forged, yet the *Arizona Daily Star* asserted, "It seems quite clear that out of the 104 votes at San Simon, most of them were fraudulent."

However, Lester F. Blackburn, a Tombstone election watchman, had an alternate viewpoint about the polling. He stated that as the votes cast for Shibell were being called, they were actually recorded as votes for Paul. In response, Paul's legal representative claimed Blackburn's statement was likely fabricated, as it could have been his revenge for Paul declining to give him a deputy sheriff commission.

Shibell scoffed at the accusation of voter fraud and demanded to present the Tombstone ballot box as evidence. Marshall Williams, the Wells Fargo agent in charge of the box, confirmed that it was in pristine condition and untampered with, just as he had last seen it.

After a close examination of the ballots, almost forty votes for Paul were revealed to have been altered. Due to the judge's ruling that all San Simon ballots were fraudulent, it was determined that the new Pima County sheriff was now Paul, with 1,684 votes in total. However, Shibell would not bow down and accept this. He filed an appeal with the Arizona Supreme Court and refused to relinquish his position as sheriff until the court delivered a decision.

The law was still deciding what would become of Paul, but he continued to drive the Wells Fargo stagecoaches. On March 15, 1881, he was on one such vehicle when it was hijacked by bandits who yelled, "Hold!" and fired shots at all aboard. Eli "Bud" Philpot was killed in the first volley of bullets, and passenger Peter Roering was wounded. Instead of stopping the wagon, Paul returned fire with a resounding "I don't hold for nobody!" and raced toward Benson to alert Wyatt Earp about the attack.

The next morning, Earp and Cochise County sheriff John H. Behan began a search for the people responsible for Philpot's death. Joined by Paul and thirty other armed men, they eventually arrested Luther King. He named Jim Crane, Harry Head and William Leonard as accomplices to the

Elections were major events that drew in crowds of people from the surrounding towns.
University of Southern California Libraries and California Historical Society.

crime. Whether or not these additional suspects were ever taken into custody is unknown. However, one thing is certain: Luther King made it out of the Tombstone jail by escaping through the back door while the undersheriff was distracted.

After the stagecoach incident, it became official: Paul was the sheriff of Pima County, as declared by the Territorial Supreme Court. After another contentious voting cycle, Paul departed the office in 1886.

Strangely, the problem of census fraud persisted in the southwestern region of Arizona, as evidenced by an article in the *Tombstone Weekly Epitaph* on August 5, 1882.

> *It is strange that the Pima County Board of Supervisors have not replied to the proposition of Cochise County regarding unity of action to prevent, if possible, the consummation of the Yavapai census fraud.*
>
> *The silence of the Pima County Commission can only be attributed to one cause, Mr. Clark Churchill, the astute northern Arizona politician, was in Tucson at the time the Pima County board received the proposition, and it is more than probable that a job was then and there effected. It has been an open secret for the past few days that Churchill promised fifteen hundred extra votes from Yavapai county to the Republican territorial ticket in consideration of passive policy regarding the census fraud by Pima and Cochise County Republicans. It has been asserted that Churchill and the leading radicals of Pima county, including the chairman of the Board of Supervisors, held long and frequent consultations and the Tucson politicians were less violent in denunciation of the fraud after each meeting.*
>
> *It is well that the people of southern Arizona should understand this deal. The Republican politicians are willing to barter away the proper representation of the southern counties in the legislative assembly in consideration of a "returning board" for the manufacture of ready-made voters, being instituted at Prescott. Such, in all probability, are the conditions of the treaty subscribed to by Clark Churchill and the Tucson Republicans. The people should bear it in mind on election day and properly repudiate the tricksters who seek to lead them into such a disgraceful alliance.*

On occasion, the political corruption turned to violence. Tombstone's two newspapers, the *Tombstone Epitaph* and the *Daily Nugget*, were politically polarized, often taking shots at each other using the written word. One such article appeared in the *Tombstone Epitaph* on December 19, 1881.

Please allow me a little space to express my views of the course pursued by the Nugget *on the cowboy question, and particularly on the attempted murder of J.P. Clum. And here first allow me to say that this letter has been read to many of our best and leading citizens, who heartily endorse every word of it.*

For a journal to make sport of and publish articles intended to be funny on such an affair as the attempted assassination of the mayor of a city is truly an outrage upon decency and an insult to the intelligence of the community. They make a joke of it and publish their slurs, but good citizens cannot look at it in that light. It is well known that no bullion goes out in the wagon on that day; neither does Kinnear's light stage carry mail or express. In fact, it was well known that the stage that night had no treasure or valuables on board. Why, then, the attempt to stop it that night, and that, too, so near to town? The fact of firing about fifteen shots into the stage and the exclamation which two of the passengers heard them make of, "Be sure and get the old bald-headed son of a b——," explains it all! They were assassins seeking to murder our mayor, and to do so, even willing to murder a stage load of passengers. If there could be any doubt of their intent, it would be at once removed by knowing of the previous threats made by the gang to murder not only the Earps but also Clum, Spicer, Williams, Fitch, and Rickenbaugh.

It is well known that the Nugget *establishment is owned by Hugo Richards of Prescott, who allows the present publishers to have the use of it on condition that they support him as a candidate for Congress. The* Nugget *has so far identified itself with the rustlers that it is generally known as the cowboy organ, and with its support, Mr. Richards will be before the people as the cowboy's candidate. Does Hugo like the platform?*

The Nugget *may think it is funny, and they are so cunning when they write their witty articles making merry over the pastime and sports of their pretty pets, such as breaking up religious services and making the preacher dance at the mouth of their revolvers, insinuating improper motives to those who oppose them, and exceedingly hilarious over a race for life made by our mayor to escape being assassinated by them. All these little pleasantries of the cowboys may be exceedingly funny graphs, may be exceedingly witty, but they will never send Hugo Richards to Congress nor reelect the present sheriff.*

The constant repetition of outrages by this gang of desperadoes known as cowboys is driving capital, capitalists, and enterprise out of the country, and for a journal published in our midst to treat these outrages with lenity is an insult to the entire community.

J.P. Clum, of course, was the proprietor of the *Tombstone Epitaph*. Because of his close ties to the Earps and his staunch support for legal business operations, he became a target for the outlaws of Cochise County—the Cowboys. Clum was certain the holdup was cover for an attempt to kill him, so he refused to reboard the stage but walked until he found a horse he could borrow and arrived in Benson the following day before traveling back to Tombstone.

In his retelling of the event, Clum recounted the attempt on his life.

> *Yes, I ran away from Tombstone. There were nine of us who were not supposed to get out of Tombstone alive. We received warnings written in blood. We didn't pay a lot of attention to them at first, but after a few months, it became most unbearable. They were picking us off one by one. We could never put our hands definitely on those who were doing it. I decided to settle elsewhere. They opened fire on me from both sides of the road. Three miles farther along the road, a bullet tore through my coat, and lead brought down my horse. I kept going without him.*

On May 1, 1882, two years after he started the *Tombstone Epitaph*, Clum sold it and left Tombstone.

Another example of the newspaper feud was published on June 10, 1882. Once again, the *Epitaph* took a shot at another local newspaper, and once again, the subject is murder.

> *The two men murdered by the Indians in South Pass, and whose mutilated bodies were brought into Tombstone, are made the subject for a horrible and brutal lie by the* Citizen. *It is asserted by that journal of advanced ideas that the killing was done by Rustlers, whoever they are, and not by savages. When it is considered that the whole affair was witnessed by three miners, who concealed themselves in the rocks, and whose testimony was given before the coroner's jury, the animus of the* Citizen's *article is easily seen. That journal, like an Ishmaelite, seems to have raised its hand against everybody and to be tested by a desire not to foster but to depreciate the resources of the Territory.*
>
> *Recognizing the demoralized condition of the Republican party in Arizona, it is desperately seeking a vent for its feelings in tales of blood and horror, conceived in fiction and bred of a diseased imagination. The* Citizen *is like a ghoulish undertaker, deriving its enjoyment from a contemplation of the dead and finding its capital in trade in the graves of murdered men.*

It has announced the issue to be made by the Republican party in this Territory as one based upon the question of whether one assassin is better than another. The Democratic party has no fight to make upon such an issue but will only advocate an impartial administration of the law, sparing none and persecuting none.

It seems that back in the Old West, bullets were not the only things used to assault those who broke the law or offended the morals of men.

CHAPTER 5
WHO KILLED JOHNNY RINGO?

The story of Wyatt Earp, his brothers and the O.K. Corral is celebrated almost daily, with tourists flocking to see the corral's famous walls. Doc Holliday even has a soda named in his memory. However, lost in these pages of history is John Peters Ringo—better known as Johnny Ringo—whose unsolved death from 134 years ago still stirs up color and debate today. He left an undeniable impact on Tombstone and on the Old West. An article in the *Tombstone Epitaph* shortly after his death on July 13, 1882, said of Ringo:

> *There are few men in Cochise County, or Southeastern Arizona, better known. He was recognized by friends and foes as a recklessly brave man who would go any distance or undergo any hardship to serve a friend or punish an enemy.*

Ringo immersed himself in the Fourth of July celebrations in 1882, guzzling alcohol and partying with his buddies. When he left Tombstone some days later, he had brought extra bottles of booze for the journey. Eventually, Ringo was seen at Dial's Ranch, located south of the Dragoons, still drinking heavily.

Soon after, he encountered Deputy Billy Breakenridge, who later wrote of the meeting:

It was shortly after noon. Ringo was very drunk, reeling in the saddle, and said he was going to Galeyville. It was in the summer and a very hot day. He offered me a drink out of a bottle half-full of whiskey, and he had another full bottle. I tasted it, and it was too hot to drink. It burned my lips. Knowing that he would have to ride nearly all night before he could reach Galeyville, I tried to get him to go back with me to the Goodrich Ranch and wait until after sundown, but he was drunk and stubborn and went on his way. I think this was the last time he was seen alive.

Around the night of July 9, Ringo was seen in Galeyville, drinking heavily. Two days later, he had moved on from town. By the afternoon of July 13, near Rustler Park, his horse had gotten loose, and he tried to chase it but didn't make it far. At around three o'clock that day, a gunshot was heard from a nearby ranch.

On July 14, 1882, teamster John Yoast discovered the body of the infamous John Ringo at the base of a tree in Arizona. Yoast, who had been acquainted with Ringo back in Texas, quickly called for help. Minutes later, other men arrived and saw that Ringo was propped up against the tree trunk. He clutched a .45-caliber Colt revolver in his right hand, and he had suffered a single gunshot wound to his right temple. The bullet had exited through the top of his head. He was buried on-site without further ado. The coroner's report suggested that Ringo's death must have been a suicide, yet others who hadn't seen the body speculated that he was murdered instead.

The men who found the deceased noted some peculiar facts about his death. His boots were missing, and strips of an undershirt were tied around his feet, suggesting he had gone for a short walk in this makeshift footwear. They also noticed his cartridge belt was upside down and saw a cut on his head with a portion of hair missing. His horse wasn't there, but it was discovered several weeks later with its saddle still attached. The people who examined him wrote a report that documented these details.

A historical photograph of Johnny Ringo taken sometime around 1880. *Wikimedia Commons.*

There was found by the undersigned John Yoast, the body of a man in a clump of Oak trees 20 yards north from the road leading to Morse's mill and about a quarter of a mile west of the house of B.F. Smith. The undersigned viewed the body and found it in a sitting posture, facing west, the head inclined to the right. There was a bullet hole in the right temple, the bullet coming out the top of the left side. There is apparently a part of the scalp gone, including a small portion of the forehead and part of the hair, this looks as if cut by a knife. These are the only marks of violence visible to the body. Several of the undersigned identify the body as that of John Ringo, well-known in Tombstone. He was dressed in a light hat, blue shirt, vest, pants, and drawers, on his feet were a pair of hose and undershirt torn up so as to protect his feet. He had evidentially traveled but a short distance in this footgear. His revolver he grasped in his right hand, his rifle rested against the tree close to him. He wore two cartridge belts. The belt for the revolver cartridges being buckled upside down.

The coroner's report, which described in detail the condition of Ringo's remains, stated:

He was dressed in a light hat, blue shirt, vest, pants and drawers. On his feet were a pair of hose [socks] and an undershirt torn up so as to protect his feet. He had evidently traveled but a short distance in this foot gear. His revolver he grasped in his right hand, his rifle resting against the tree close to him. He had on two cartridge belts, the belt for revolver cartridges being buckled on upside down. The under-noted property was found with him and on his person: one Colt's revolver, caliber 45, No. 222, containing five cartridges; one Winchester rifle octagon barrel, caliber 45, model 1876, No. 21,986, containing a cartridge in the breech and ten in the magazine; 1 cartridge belt, containing 9 rifle cartridges; 1 cartridge belt, containing 2 revolver cartridges; 1 silver watch of American Watch Company, No. 9339, with silver chain attached; two dollars and sixty cents ($2.60) in money; 6 pistol cartridges in pocket; 5 shirt studs; 1 small pocket knife; 1 tobacco pipe; 1 comb; 1 block matches; 1 small piece tobacco. There is also a portion of a letter from Messrs. Hereford & Zabriskie, attorneys at law, Tucson, to the deceased, John Ringo.

Ringo appeared to have passed away the day before, and he was quickly laid to rest in Turkey Creek near Chiricahua Peak. The site where he was found is still near Sanders Ranch, approximately ninety minutes from Tombstone by car today. What happened there that caused Ringo to receive that fatal wound remains a mystery. Over the years, various explanations

Johnny Ringo's grave near Turkey Creek. *Photo by author.*

and potential perpetrators have been suggested by researchers to explain the events that occurred.

The initial suspect was "Buckskin" Frank Leslie, who had a reputation for violence even among the notorious outlaws of the time. Multiple clues point to the potential that he could be the one responsible for killing John Ringo.

In 1880, Leslie opened the Cosmopolitan Hotel in Tombstone. Not long after, it was said that he killed a man in self-defense during an altercation concerning the man's wife. He also reputedly brutally beat someone outside the Oriental Saloon. Even though the police could not confirm his involvement when it happened, Leslie's role in Ringo's demise became more apparent over time as more evidence surfaced.

Leslie and Claiborne, who were pals of Ringo's, got into a heated dispute in Tombstone in 1882. In the November edition of the *Tombstone Epitaph*, it was said that Claiborne informed his buddies he was going to shoot Leslie "for killing John Ringo." Subsequently, Claiborne left the Oriental Saloon—where Leslie worked as a barman—after warning him and returned with a gun. They met face-to-face on Allen Street, immediately outside the tavern, and Leslie shot Claiborne dead, almost four months after Ringo had passed away. According to reports from the *Epitaph*, on his deathbed, Claiborne said, "Frank Leslie murdered John Ringo. I helped him carry Ringo in there."

Additionally, the Cochise County Historical and Archaeological Society's *Cochise Quarterly* newsletter from 1973, by Archie L. Gee, mentions that Leslie confessed to shooting Ringo almost ten years after his death. Leslie was held in the Yuma Penitentiary for murdering a harmless prostitute in 1889, and while he was there, he told a guard about his showdown with Ringo at Turkey Creek Canyon. According to Leslie, Ringo fired first, and he shot back in self-defense—apparently fatally wounding Ringo.

Nashville Franklyn "Buckskin Frank" Leslie, a lawman, U.S. Army scout, gambler and outlaw of the American Old West. *Wikimedia Commons.*

Leslie was released from prison after seven years and relocated to the City of San Francisco in 1904. However, the date and cause of his death remain a mystery. Though details about why Leslie murdered Ringo remain unknown, historians claim that there is significant evidence proving his guilt.

Another potential suspect is Wyatt Earp, one of the most renowned lawmen in the Wild West. It was rumored that he confessed to being Johnny Ringo's killer. He had plenty of reason to take out Ringo, as his clashes with the cowboys from Tombstone have gone down as legendary moments in U.S. history. Author W.C. Jameson writes in his 1999 book *Unsolved Mysteries of the Old West*:

> *It is well known that the two men hated one another and either would likely have taken advantage of any opportunity to kill the other.*

In 1932, three years after Wyatt Earp died in Los Angeles at the age of eighty, a writer named Frank Lockwood published his book *Pioneer Days in Arizona*. According to Lockwood, he had interviewed Wyatt, and Earp recounted in detail how he killed John Ringo. Another researcher/writer, John D. Gilchriese, also produced a hand-drawn map supposedly sketched from memory by Earp to depict where he murdered Ringo.

At the time of Ringo's death, Earp was residing in Colorado. Nevertheless, many stories exist about how he could have managed to reach Turkey Creek on July 13, 1882. Gilchriese mapped out a proposed path to the crime scene and back, noting which train routes were accessible and how long the journey was—as well as subsequent horseback rides from East

Las Vegas to Roswell to Lordsburg and then straight into the Chiricahuas to Turkey Creek. He calculated that it would have taken approximately six days on horseback and one by train. Once he finished his calculations, Gilchriese told the *Arizona Daily Star* in 1964 that Earp could have made his way from Colorado to the Chiricahuas without being noticed, killed Ringo and returned right after that.

Alternative accounts credit Michael O'Rourke as the one who brought Ringo's life to an end. He was arrested in Tucson at the beginning of 1881 for allegedly taking the life of a mining engineer called Henry Schneider. According to these stories, Wyatt Earp protected O'Rourke from being lynched by a mob assembled by Ringo himself. O'Rourke managed to break free from jail in April that same year and never faced trial for murder.

The last confirmed sighting of O'Rourke was in the Dragoon Mountains close to Tombstone during May 1881, "well-equipped and mounted." After that, all we have are rumors and legends about him. According to one story, his debt to Earp and his grudge against Ringo drove him back to Arizona in 1882 to seek revenge on Ringo. While some believe this story to be accurate, others mention how unlikely it would have been for O'Rourke, like Holliday, to risk reentering Arizona with a murder warrant hanging over his head just to commit another murder.

Today, the accepted cause of death for John "Ringo" is suicide with a .45-caliber Colt. This notion isn't just speculation but is definitively recognized as an official explanation.

William M. Breakenridge served as the right-hand man of Sheriff John Behan in Tombstone and was close to both lawmen and cowboys. He was one of the last people to see Ringo alive, and in 1928—some forty-six years after Ringo's death—Breakenridge documented their meeting in his memoir *Helldorado: Bringing the Law to the Mesquite*. In it, he described Ringo as "drunk" when he saw him and speculated that Ringo must have laid down to rest once his drinking had taken its toll. After finding out that Ringo's horse had wandered away (which was true) and that his final resting place was near Turkey Creek (also true), Breakenridge surmised that Ringo became desperate for water and went looking for it on foot. Apparently, he got so thirsty that he ended up killing himself while still within earshot of running water.

In his 1980 book *John Ringo: The Story of a Western Myth*, author Jack Burrows speculates that John Ringo's death was an act of suicide brought on by depression. He concluded that there had been "no escape from himself."

Alternative ideas about Ringo's death have been suggested throughout the decades, one of which is that Doc Holliday was the one who ended Ringo's life in Turkey Creek. The 1993 movie *Tombstone* has a scene that shows this happening. But if it were true, Holliday would have had to be a master criminal to pull off the feat. Records from a Colorado courtroom show he was in court for larceny on July 11 and 14, 1882—two days before and one day after Ringo died on July 13. Meanwhile, many researchers point to flaws in the other, even more credible, theories.

The Earp theory, based mainly on the purported map drawn by Wyatt depicting where he killed and left Ringo, has discrepancies. The site where Ringo was found to have perished doesn't match Earp's description. Additionally, Lockwood's book is generally deemed unreliable.

John Gilchriese, a researcher looking into Wyatt Earp during the 1960s, suggested to a reporter that Earp could have made his way from Colorado to Arizona and killed Ringo in approximately six days. While this scenario was within Earp's capabilities, the idea of him making such an incredible journey seemed implausible. Soon after, Glenn Boyer, a controversial author who published three books and several articles about Wyatt Earp, provided an account of how Earp supposedly killed Ringo from the perspective of Wyatt's wife, Josie Earp. However, this story contained inaccuracies—for instance, Doc Holliday and Fred Dodge being part of the group that killed Ringo, while Dodge's own words disprove this point. Dodge, an undercover detective employed by Wells Fargo in Arizona at the time, shared his story with author Stuart Lake. He claims that Johnny-Behind-the-Deuce (Michael O'Rourke) was responsible for Ringo's death.

The idea that Ringo committed suicide is called into question by certain forensic aspects of the case that have also puzzled researchers. According to the coroner's report, there was an entry hole in Ringo's right temple, and the bullet exited out of the top left of his skull, indicating an upward path for the projectile. However, when Ringo's corpse was found, his hat was still on his head, with no bullet holes or other signs of violence. This inconsistency has kept investigators looking for new answers.

The coroner's jury also noted that Ringo's gun was holding five cartridges. This led many to theorize that the weapon hadn't been used yet. There was no indication in the coroner's report of whether any rounds had been shot off. During this period, it was typical for only five rounds to be put into a pistol as a safety measure to avoid an accidental discharge if the firing pin rested on a live round. Nevertheless, it was known that some people carried six bullets in their guns. For instance, Wyatt Earp in Wichita and "Curly Bill" Brocius both had their weapons fire when they fell from their belts and struck the ground. So, although it was a common practice to load just five bullets into a pistol, several people loaded six rounds into theirs. Therefore, the coroner's jury's report is compatible with the idea that Ringo's gun contained one spent round. In fact, these men must have realized that he could not have taken his own life if there were no fired cartridges in his pistol.

Many people also thought that the lack of powder burns on Ringo's face and head meant he couldn't have committed suicide. Years later, Henry Smith—the son of one of the men who discovered the body—allegedly claimed that he didn't see any powder burns on the body. Robert Boller—another man who had found Ringo's body—wrote decades after the event that "the body had turned black" when they discovered it. Although we should be careful when considering Boller's comments, due to the long time that had passed since he saw the body, if his account is accurate, it would have been near impossible to make out the powder burns on Ringo's face because of how badly deteriorated his body was. After all, he had been lying in the hot July sun for almost a day.

Years later, Boller composed a letter to Frank King in which he recounted the tragic scene of Ringo's death:

> *I showed him* [Yoast] *where the bullet had entered the tree on the left side. Blood and brains oozing from the wound and matted his hair. There was an empty shell in the six-shooter, and the hammer was on that. I called it suicide fifty-two years ago, and I am still calling it suicide. I guess I'm the last of the coroner's jury.*

Boller's statements seemed to discredit the two theories that had been circulating. Boller reported an empty cartridge still in the gun and a hole in the tree where the bullet had gone after hitting Ringo's head. It was clear that even shortly after Ringo's death, no one could explain what had happened.

An *Epitaph* article published at the time mentioned that those who knew Ringo were divided on the cause of his death, with some believing it was not self-inflicted and others pointing to reports of him threatening suicide in the past. It was as if they were expecting the event to occur at any moment.

Many amateur researchers and historians acknowledge that it's unlikely they'll ever determine the exact cause of Ringo's death with absolute certainty. But several are still asking the Cochise County Sheriff's Office to reopen the case and consider changing the official cause of Johnny Ringo's death from suicide to "undetermined."

CHAPTER 6
AT THE END OF A ROPE

Hangings in Tombstone could be legal or illegal, based on the situation and the person. The environment in Tombstone was rough, and punishments were correspondingly harsh. People wanted for their crimes could be sought by the authorities or citizens determined to practice justice in a lawless land.

The gallows acted as a source of morbid amusement. It brought together people from all corners of the area who wanted to take photos of what was left behind. Viewing an Old West hanging was a way for spectators to be reminded of the law and served as an escape from their regular lives. These events proved that sticking by the frontier rules—no matter how murky they could be—was best for everyone watching. Frontier hangings taught those in attendance that life could be much worse than what they were living through.

Eight of the ten hangings that took place in the "Town Too Tough to Die" were legal executions of convicted felons. The other two were executions by lynch mobs. Of the eight legal hangings, two would end the lives of eight men.

The first occurred on February 22, 1884. Five men were about to face their execution in Tombstone, Arizona. As the rope was tightened around their necks, the last words heard from the gallows were, "Let her loose." Dan Kelly shouted this before his fate was sealed by the trapdoor below him. The Irishman had been in America for less than three years before he died in Tombstone.

At the age of twenty-one, Dan Kelly set sail from Cork, looking for an improved life in the United States of America. After arriving in New

The old gallows at the Tombstone Courthouse National Historic Park in 1946. *Library of Congress.*

York Harbor from Queenstown, he traveled to Clifton, Arizona, where he encountered other Irish immigrants. During his journey, he got involved with some cowboy outlaws and eventually became part of the group that committed the Bisbee Massacre in December 1883.

Bisbee, a mining town, did not have a bank, but it did have the Goldwater and Castaneda Mercantile, which owned a strongbox. Every night, miners would deposit their salaries in that box. On December 8, 1883, five masked bandits came to town determined to steal the money inside the safe. They planned to swoop in at eight o'clock, when they assumed $7,000 worth of payroll would be stored there, but they ended up arriving too early and causing an uproar.

The tombstone of the men who were hanged for their participation in the Bisbee Massacre. *Library of Congress.*

John Heath, a dubious character from Texas, was the one who planned the robbery without taking part. He relocated to Bisbee with his pal James "Tex" Howard in November 1883 and became friendly with Dan Dowd, Red Sample, William Delaney and Dan "Yorkie" Kelly. As for Heath himself, he had previously been involved in some shady activities such as stealing cattle, thieving and owning a bordello.

On the night of December 8, the thieves rode into town and secured their horses to a post at the end of the main drag. Three of them entered the store, while two remained outside as lookouts with their guns drawn. To the surprise of everyone inside, they demanded that the employees open the safe—ironically, the paychecks had not been delivered yet, so all that was inside was just a few hundred dollars.

On the sidewalk, passersby noticed something was occurring in the general store and demanded that the two criminals manning the front entrance step aside. J.C. Tappenier was one of those who challenged them, and unfortunately, he sustained a gunshot wound for his courageousness.

Sheriff Tom Smith had been dining at the restaurant across from the store when he heard the ruckus and sprinted over to investigate. Unfortunately, he was struck by a bullet in the process. Anne Roberts, who owned the restaurant and was pregnant, opened the door to see what had happened—only to be taken down by another bullet. All of this together would later become known as the Bisbee Massacre.

As he arrived in town, John Nolly, a key witness to the crime, found himself in the midst of mayhem and quickly jumped under his wagon for safety. The robbery had descended into a chaotic scene of violence, with the robbers shooting wildly at the end of the street before running back to their horses, injuring multiple people.

After the robbers galloped away, a bounty was announced for their capture. A posse was quickly put together, and to everyone's surprise, John Heath tagged along. The posse followed the trail of the men they sought, but

Boothill Graveyard in 1940, before it was fully restored. *Library of Congress.*

Heath attempted to throw them off. Heath's deception resulted in the group splitting up, yet they still successfully apprehended their quarry.

Tex Howard, a known companion of Heath, was the first person captured; he was identified quickly, as he was the only one who hadn't put on a mask. Attention then shifted to Heath, who was also taken into custody. Dan Kelly disguised himself as a hobo on a train but was still spotted in New Mexico and taken back to Arizona in chains. Delaney was the final suspect to be apprehended, after a brawl at a bar. He was identified as one of the people responsible for the Bisbee Massacre.

In February 1884, Heath, Dowd, Sample, Kelly and Delaney stood trial in Tombstone. The hearing lasted for three days until all the men were found guilty and sentenced to death by hanging, save for Heath, who was given a life sentence.

The public was outraged, and a mob descended on the county jail where Heath had been locked up. They dragged him out into the street and tied a rope around his neck at a telegraph pole on Toughnut Street. In his final moments, Heath's last words were, "I have one favor to ask. That you will not mutilate my body by shooting into it after I am hung."

Heath's remains were laid to rest in Boothill Graveyard, but his family later requested that they be exhumed and shipped to Texas. His final resting place remains unmarked, but a grave marker remains where he was initially buried in Boothill.

Leading up to their executions, a reporter was allowed to talk with the convicted men. During the conversation, Kelly declared boldly, "I will walk upright to the gallows."

The hangings made national news and attracted crowds to the town to watch the spectacle. Local businesses saw an opportunity to profit from this morbid occasion, including one businessman who constructed a grandstand and charged $1.50 for the best seats in the house. However, not everyone was comfortable with how the hangings were to be conducted, and Nellie Cashman, a native of Cork, took issue with it.

Nellie Cashman was born in Middleton, Ireland, in 1845. Five years later, she and her family migrated to the United States, seeking a better life. On arriving in the Wild West, Cashman earned the nickname Angel of Tombstone for her kindness toward miners and immigrants. She even became close with Dan Kelly. In the days leading up to his execution, Father Patrick Gallagher—the parish priest of Tombstone, who was also an Irish immigrant—helped Cashman care for the condemned men.

On the day of the hanging, Cashman enlisted some miners to help her. They took an axe to the grandstand and tore it apart, which caused a fight to break out in the streets. People were injured as a result, including one person with a broken leg and another with a fractured arm. Nellie Cashman got her wish: what was left of the grandstand was in ruins, and no tickets were sold for the event.

A huge crowd gathered on the day of the executions in Tombstone to see the spectacle of Old West justice. The doomed prisoners were well-groomed and wearing identical black suits, and at 1:18 p.m. on March 28, 1884, they were finally hanged. Kelly shouted, in his heavy Cork accent, "Let her loose," and instantly, they dropped from the gallows. Everyone but Dowd died immediately; he struggled for a few minutes until the noose eventually choked him.

JOHN HEITH, lynched on Feb. 22, 1884, by infuriated citizens in Arizona.

The lynching of John Heath at Tombstone, Arizona, February 22, 1884. He was implicated in the robbery of the Goldwater & Castaneda store in December 1883, wherein three men and one woman were killed. The other five men involved were apprehended and legally hanged at Tombstone on March 6, 1884. *Library of Congress.*

A historical photograph of the grave of John Heath in Boothill Graveyard. Taken in 1939.
Library of Congress.

Nellie Cashman hired miners to guard the corpses from body snatchers and ghoulish souvenir hunters. For ten days, they guarded the bodies in the town morgue before they were buried in Boothill Graveyard, where they remain to this day.

THE ILL-FATED SHOOTOUT AT Wilson Ranch concluded with the most notorious hanging to ever take place in Tombstone. On April 7, 1899, two lawmen came face-to-face with brothers William and Thomas Lee Halderman at a ranch located in the Chiricahua Mountains. A brief shootout broke out, in which Constable Chester L. Ainsworth was killed and his deputy, Teddy Moore, severely wounded. The Halderman brothers then ran off to New Mexico but were quickly apprehended and brought to trial in Tombstone. On November 16, 1900, their death sentences were carried out.

The Halderman brothers, William and Thomas, tragically passed away before they could reach the ages of twenty-two and nineteen. Although from a well-to-do family of Texan settlers known as the Kokernots, they had taken to working as cowboys in Cochise County, Arizona.

In 1898, Teddy Moore and the Halderman brothers were at odds over two young ladies, Rena and Mary Wilson. Moore allegedly threatened

William's life on more than one occasion during the months leading up to April 6, 1899. That day, Buck Smith, owner of the local ranch, reported to Justice William Monmonier that the Halderman siblings had been stealing and killing his cattle. Monmonier promptly issued a warrant, and Constable Chester Ainsworth was sent out to make the arrest.

In 1899, the Chiricahua Mountains were a remote and untamed place. Constable Ainsworth was dispatched from his office in Pearce to ask one of the ranchers at Smith Ranch for assistance in capturing the notorious Haldermans. Smith denied the constable's request for help and instructed him to carry on to Teddy Moore's house, which was less than a mile from the Moore Ranch.

Ainsworth went there, and after deputizing Moore, they headed to the Halderman Ranch, which was situated a short way off, near Turkey Creek Canyon. Finding the house empty, Ainsworth and Moore regrouped and decided to investigate the Wilson Ranch. It was owned by John W. Wilson; his two sons, Johnny and Tol; and his daughters, Rena and Mary, who lived on the property.

On the morning of April 7, 1899, just after sunrise, Constable Ainsworth and Teddy Moore rode up to the Wilson house. The two lawmen stood approximately forty feet from the front porch. Ainsworth then yelled out the arrest warrant for the Halderman brothers and asked them to come outside in peace.

It appeared that the two young men would give in without a fight, and Ainsworth recommended they have breakfast before departing and collect some of their belongings for an extended stay in Pearce. But while inside the house, the Haldermans determined that Moore wanted to hurt them instead of taking them into custody, so they got weapons and came out through both entrances of the home, positioned at opposite ends of the porch.

William grabbed the family's rifle, and his brother took Mr. Wilson's. As soon as both William and his brother shouldered their weapons, the lawmen opened fire. William immediately began shooting back, and after he shot off all his ammunition, he ran across the porch to get his brother's gun and continued shooting at Moore.

Unfortunately, during this time, Ainsworth was shot from his horse and killed, struck directly in the heart by a bullet. William later insisted that Ainsworth's death was an accident because he got caught in the crossfire. William believed that Moore was going to kill him and his brother and thus he was their sole target.

As Ainsworth hit the ground, Moore wheeled his horse around and began to gallop away from the house as fast as he could. However, William was in pursuit, and at a distance of about 150 yards, he managed to fire off one more shot that struck Moore in the bowels with deadly accuracy. Despite being mortally wounded, Moore was able to make it back to his ranch, where he spent a few hours bleeding out in his mother's arms before passing away.

Before his passing, Moore was able to tell his family the story of what happened. He claimed that the Haldermans shot first, and the Wilson sisters initially agreed with him because their father threatened to punish them if they said anything else. It wasn't until after the Haldermans were sentenced to death that the Wilson sisters spoke up and revealed what happened. Unfortunately, there was nothing anyone could do about it.

The following appeared in the *Pacific Reporter*, volume 60:

> *It appears from the record that on April 6, 1899, a complaint was lodged before W.* [William] *M. Monmonier, a justice of the peace for the precinct of Pearce, Cochise County, charging the Haldermans with having unlawfully killed cattle. A warrant was issued by the justice upon this complaint and placed in the hands of one C.* [Chester] *L. Ainsworth, constable of the precinct, and a deputy sheriff* [Teddy Moore] *of the county.... They then went to the house of a neighbor by the name of* [John W.] *Wilson, where they found the defendants. Ainsworth and Moore rode to the front of the Wilson house, dismounted from their horses, and called the Haldermans out, whereupon Ainsworth read his warrant of arrest to them. Both Haldermans expressed a willingness to go with the officer, but before starting, upon suggestion of the latter* [Ainsworth], *went into the house to get their breakfast. While they were inside, Ainsworth called to them and told them, as they might be detained at Pierce* [Pearce] *for two or three days, to take with them such articles of wearing apparel* [clothing] *as they might need. Soon after, the Haldermans appeared, one at each of the two front doors of the house, armed with rifles, and at once opened fire, instantly killing Ainsworth and mortally wounding Moore. As to the facts above stated, there is no substantial conflict in the evidence. The testimony of the witness for the prosecution, supported by the dying declaration of Moore, as to the circumstances of the shooting, is to the effect that at the time the Haldermans appeared at the doors, Ainsworth and Moore were both mounted, and a short distance from the house; that the Haldermans, as soon as they appeared, called to Ainsworth and Moore to hold up their hands, but without waiting, at once fired; that Ainsworth immediately fell*

The Tombstone Courthouse, constructed of red brick in 1882. *Library of Congress.*

from his horse, shot through the heart; that Moore turned his horse, and started off, but was shot through the bowels as he rode away; that after the shooting the Haldermans immediately fled. The story, as told by the defendants, was that between themselves and Moore had existed a deadly enmity; that, after the warrant had been read, they asked the constable how they were to be taken to Pierce; that they were then told that they would have to walk down to a neighboring ranch, where there was a conveyance of some sort; that, fearing that Moore might on some pretext seek occasion on the way down to the ranch to do them [the Halderman brothers] *harm, they concluded while in the house to take their rifles with them; that, as soon as they appeared at the front of the house, Moore pulled his gun and fired; that William Halderman at once returned the fire, and continued shooting until he had emptied his gun, and, as Moore continued to shoot, he then ran to the other door, where his brother Thomas Halderman stood, and, seizing the latter's gun, fired again at Moore, but by accident killed Ainsworth; that, fearing* [lynch] *mob violence at the hands of the friends of Ainsworth, the two then left the county.*

The day after the shooting, the sheriff of Cochise County, Scott White, announced that those who apprehended the Haldermans would be given a fifty-dollar reward. The poster detailing this offer was distributed widely. Despite the small amount of money being offered, on April 12, Deputy Sid Mullen tracked them down to their camping spot just east of Duncan, right by the New Mexico border.

The Haldermans were first incarcerated in Pearce then transferred to Tombstone for their trial. By early June, they had been found guilty of murder in the first degree and sentenced to hang on August 10, 1900.

The Halderman family was determined to clear their name in the courts and prevent a stain on their reputation as one of the best pioneer families of Texas. Although they were not successful, they did manage to gain an extension on the hanging. During this time, the family searched for evidence that could help prove that Buck Smith's claims of cattle rustling were false and that the shootout actually resulted from a feud rather than simply a crime of theft.

The Haldermans accused Moore of stealing their cattle and attempting to frame them in order to court Rena Wilson. They requested a stay of execution, which Governor Nathan O. Murphy was unable to grant due to his absence. So the plea was presented to President William McKinley, who agreed and postponed the execution until October 5, 1900, so they could find more proof to defend themselves.

When he returned, Governor Murphy extended the stay for the Haldermans, but they failed to produce their evidence, and a date for their execution was set: November 16, 1900. The Kokernot-Halderman family complained that they didn't get a fair trial since the prosecutor was none other than Charles L. Ainsworth, brother of Chester Ainsworth, and all twelve members of the jury were hoping for a hanging.

The execution was held on November 16, as agreed. Many people were present for the hanging, though only one hundred individuals had received official invitations. The rest observed from the windows of the Old Cochise County Courthouse. Reports suggest that both Haldermans demonstrated courage in their final moments.

When Thomas Halderman appeared from the jail, he said: "Hello, hombres….The sun's hot, ain't it?" After climbing up the scaffold, William said: "Nice-looking crowd. Some of you fellers are shaking already." Then, as he turned to his brother, William said: "Those people look alright."

Just after that, Thomas placed a hangman's rope around his neck while Sheriff White read the execution order and William conversed with Deputy

The grave of George Johnson in Boothill Graveyard. *Library of Congress.*

Bravin. When Sheriff White finished reading, he asked the Haldermans if they had any final speeches they wished to make. William responded: "I have nothing to say and guess it would not do any good anyway. I forgive you all and hope you will forgive me." William asked for a moment to pray, so Reverend Alexander Elliott stepped forward to support him. The executioners then draped masks over the Haldermans' faces, and they said in unison, "Goodbye boys! Pray for us."

At precisely 12:40 p.m., the floor beneath the Haldermans suddenly opened up and swallowed them both. By 1:03 p.m., Thomas had already been pronounced dead due to a broken neck, and two minutes after that, William passed away from "the violent shock, compression of a vital nerve, and by strangulation."

The Halderman brothers were the last outlaws to be buried in Boothill Graveyard in Tombstone, and their graves are still open to visitors. The Old Cochise County Courthouse has been reconstructed to appear as it did during the Haldermans' trial in 1900.

The Wilson family's fate was dark and twisted. Rena's guilt in the case ate away at her until she took her own life, and in 1913, Mary was confined to an insane asylum by her brother Tol, who was killed shortly after that in a violent act known as the Cottonwood Canyon Murder. The whole tale is one of heartbreak and tragedy.

CHAPTER 7

THE OTHER GUNFIGHT AT THE O.K. CORRAL

I n 1897, Jim Burnett hired a team of Chinese laborers to build a dam on the San Pedro River in order to secure more water for his crops and livestock. In addition, he directed the laborers to demolish a nearby dam owned by William C. Greene that was also blocking the river's flow.

On June 24, 1897, Greene's dam was destroyed. Three days later, his young daughters, Ella and Eva Greene, accompanied by their friend Edna Cochran, arrived at the familiar swimming spot they had always visited. To their horror, the explosion had changed the river's flow and increased its forcefulness. Where once lay a shallow pool to splash around in, now a steep, deep hole was laid with an unforgiving undercurrent. Edna leaped in before they could stop her. Ella jumped in, too, and screamed for her sister to "Go back, go back!" Eva ran off to get help, but it was too late. Ella and Edna were swept away and drowned. Greene was devastated. He soon found out who was responsible—Burnett—and went out looking for him.

What happened next was reported in the *Tombstone Epitaph* on July 1, 1897:

> *Once more has Tombstone asserted herself as a sensation producer. This time, the sensation involved another human life. W.C. Greene shot and killed James C. Burnett on Allen Street.*
>
> *This afternoon, about one o'clock, the total quiet of the city was disturbed by the report of a shot followed by three more, apparently in the same direction on Allen Street.*

A Prospector *reporter was on the ground within a few seconds, and in the midst of a crowd of excited spectators lay the body of James C. Burnett face downward in a pool of blood. When the body was turned over, the last heaving of the lungs caused gouts of blood to be spent from a ghastly wound in the breast.*

All was excitement and confusion. At this moment, Sheriff Scott White appeared, and Chief of Police Wiser, to whom Greene had surrendered, delivered the prisoner to him, and he was conducted to jail.

Coroner Jas. Dancea impaneled a jury who, after examining the body, retired to the city hall to hear the evidence in the case.

The origin of the tragedy dates immediately from the destruction of the dam of Greene, which caused the death by drowning of his little daughter and her playmate, Edna Cochran. After the destruction of Greene's dam, the dam of Burnett was also destroyed, and when Burnett came to the city yesterday, it was with the intention of going to his ranch to investigate.

Greene left the city yesterday evening in his buggy, accompanied by Sheriff White, bound for the ranch. He returned again this morning, and nothing unusual was observed in his demeanor before the shooting occurred.

A *Prospector* reporter visited Greene in the sheriff's office a few minutes after the shooting and asked him if he had any statement to make. He said,

I have no statement to make other than that man was the cause of my child being drowned. I ascertained beyond the shadow of a doubt that he was the guilty man, and when I thought of my little girl as she put her arms around my neck on the day she was drowned, I could think of nothing but vengeance on the man that caused her death. I have lived in this territory for twenty-five years and have always been a peaceable, law-abiding man. I held no animosity and have no regret for anything except the death of my little girl and the little Cochran girl and the grief of my poor wife.

He added, "Vengeance is mine, I will repay, saith the Lord."

Greene came into the *Prospector* office on the twenty-eighth and had a notice inserted in the paper offering a reward of $1,000 for proof of the identity of the person who destroyed his dam and thereby caused the death by drowning of his daughter and her little companion. He said very little at the time but seemed deeply affected and showed signs of grief.

Both Barnett and Greene were well known throughout the county, having been pioneers before the creation of Cochise County. Barnett, at the time of his death, was justice of the peace at Pearce and owned a ranch on the San Pedro near the ranch of W.C. Greene. A chance word revealed the fact that relations between the two men had not been of the most friendly character for a long time past, with Greene accusing Barnett of trying to injure him in different ways.

The most important witness sworn was John Montgomery, who testified in court that when Greene came into town with Scott White, he came to Montgomery's stable and asked that his team be put up and also left his pistol with Montgomery.

I locked it up, and later, just before the shooting, probably two hours later, he asked me if there was anyone working in Hart's old shop. I told him there was; he intimated to me his pistol needed repairs, and he wanted to have it repaired. I started to get it for him, as the room was occupied at that time, and I told him he would have to wait a few minutes before I could get it. He talked of the weather for a few minutes about rain, then I got a chair for him to sit down until I could get the pistol. He sat down. Perhaps five or ten minutes after he spoke about the pistol, I went and got it for him. I gave it to him, and he had apparently started, as I supposed, for the shop, but he did not put it in his pocket as far I saw; he turned around by the corner of the office and accused Jim Burnett of having his (Greene's) dam blown up; the words I don't remember. Burnett made denial in words which I do not remember, and just then, there were three shots fired, one immediately following another by Wm. Greene. I saw him with his pistol in his hand. I saw him elevate the pistol, and three shots immediately followed. There was another, I think after Burnett fell. Burnett came through the front door of the office, apparently very badly wounded, and went on the sidewalk probably forty feet, more or less, and then fell. Burnett had been sitting for some time in the inside of the office. I heard no words of Burnett except the disclaimer to the accusation of Greene. The jury of inquest found that the deceased came to his death by pistol shot wounds inflicted by William C. Greene.

The *New York Sun* published an article on September 17, 1897, which gave more details on the incident and the men involved.

Jim Burnett, Justice of the Peace at Pearce Camp, who was shot and killed at Tombstone, Ariz., on July 1 by William Greene, a rival ranchman, was an old New York boy. He was born at Eighteenth Street and Eighth Avenue, in the Sixteenth ward, and his family and relatives were well known on the west side of town years ago. He was 69 years old when he was killed. He left his home in this city when a lad of 19.

He was of a wild, restless disposition but also hard-headed and chock-full of pluck and determination. He went to California first and remained there for several years. Then, his roving temperament asserted itself, and he rambled around through the mining camps in the West until he settled down in Arizona. The story told about him in the Sun *on Wednesday of last week was characteristic of him. He was one of the early settlers in Charleston, on the San Pedro River, in Arizona, when that mining town was a community of desperadoes. He was made Justice of the Peace, and when the County Supervisors cut down his fees by one-half, he just quit sending in bills and financial returns and punished all offenders by fining them and pocketed the fines. He fined a man $1,000 for killing another man and declined to issue appeal papers. When the man consulted a lawyer, the latter advised him to pay and skip out. It was said that Burnett made $22,000 in this way.*

Henry Burnett, Lieutenant of Engine Company 19 in this city, is a brother of the late Justice of the Peace Burnett. Lieut. Burnett had heard from his brother in the West only at intervals of years. When Jim was killed, Lieut. Burnett wrote to his brother's friends at Tombstone asking for particulars, and from the replies that he received, it appears that civilization has not altogether prevailed over wild Western methods at Tombstone.

Another letter was from P.B. Warnekros of Tombstone and read as follows:

I am glad to hear from you and will give you such details as I know. I had known and done business with your brother for the last twelve years when he was contractor at Fort Huachuca, about twenty-four miles from here. I used to supply him, and our business relations have always been pleasant. I always found him strictly honorable in all his dealings. He married a Mexican woman about nineteen years ago. She had a family there of three grown girls, of which he was very fond and always provided for them the best he could. He bought a ranch on the San Pedro River about thirty miles from Tombstone, which he gave to his wife, and he gave her all the money he made to invest in it. He lived most of the time at Fort Huachuca, where he had beef, wood, hay, and mail contracts.

This man, W.C. Greene, that murdered poor Jim, owns a ranch on the river adjoining that owned by Jim. Greene was accused by Jim's wife of

It is rather odd that the gunfight that actually happened at the O.K. Corral is not very well known. Arizona reenactors Aaron Gain, Zach Etter, Kyle Truhill and Bob Kenney relive the "Town Too Tough to Die" days of the 1880s, when western legends such as Wyatt Earp and John Henry "Doc" Holliday walked Tombstone's streets. *Library of Congress.*

stealing and killing her cattle, and this started bad feeling between the two families. Greene rented about forty acres of his land to some Chinamen for vegetable gardening and got a big rent. The Chinamen dissolved, and Jim rented one part of his ranch. They became rivals. Jim's Chinamen raised fine crops this year, which made Greene envious.

About the middle of June, Greene's daughters and another girl and Greene's stepdaughter's husband went to the dam near Jim's ranch to fish. They fished with giant powder, the young man throwing the powder in and the girls wading in afterward and catching the fish as they came to the surface. They enjoyed themselves for some time, and when it was time to go home, the two older girls requested the young man to go ahead with the younger girl, saying they would follow later as they wanted to take a swim on the other side of the dam. He went along home, and when the two girls did not get home in a reasonable time, he and others set out in search of them. They found their bodies at the bottom of the river. One had evidently lost her footing and fell in the river, and the other had tried to save her, as both had all their clothes on. Greene was away at the time, and when he returned, he visited the scene of the drowning and found a stick of the powder his son-in-law had been using.

Greene at once proclaimed that Jim had blown up his dam with powder and drowned his girls. He thought such a report would justify him in doing what he then had on his mind. He went to the Chinaman that had leased Jim's land and compelled him at the point of his revolver to break and destroy Jim's dam in five or six places and then threatened to kill all the Chinamen if they did not leave. Jim was at this time running a store for me in Pearce camp about twenty-eight miles from here and sixty miles from his ranch.

The Chinaman telegraphed for him to come home, telling what had happened. Jim's wife came in and met him coming into Tombstone. Jim had papers made out for Greene's arrest for destroying his damn. This was on June 30. On the morning of July 1, the sheriff came in with Greene. He was taken to the Justice's Court, and the trial was set for that afternoon. Greene knew that Jim would make him pay for all damage done to his land by destroying the dam; besides, he had damaged all the other ranches along the river, and it exasperated him so that he thought he would kill Jim and allow the public to think he did it to avenge the death of the girls that were drowned.

Jim had no idea that Greene would attack him in the manner he did, for when they met in the morning, Greene commenced to abuse Jim in the street. Jim told him to stop that abuse and said that if he wished to settle the trouble personally with him, he could step out of town, and he would give him satisfaction. Greene declined. So, about 1 o'clock, after Jim had had his lunch, he sat down outside of a stable and lit his pipe. He had just been talking with our Supervisor when Greene stepped out of the office in the stable, turned around, faced Jim, and shot him while he was sitting down. Jim must have gotten up, for it was several seconds before he fired the second shot, and as he fired the third shot, Jim ran about ten feet and fell on the sidewalk. Greene walked out and down the street. He turned and noticed Jim lying down on the sidewalk. He came back, stooped over Jim, hunted a vital spot, and deliberately shot him again.

My store is only a short distance from the stable, and my wife was the first to run out. She saw Greene fire the last shot, and when she heard whom he had killed, she flew toward Greene and begged the people to tear him limb from limb. She then went to poor Jim and turned him over and lifted his head, but poor Jim was dead. He never spoke after he *was hit, and his pipe lay beside him. He had not even a pocket knife on him. Greene delivered himself to an officer who had run to the scene and was taken to jail. He enjoyed every liberty and freedom, as the sheriff is a personal friend of his. We had poor Jim buried the next day, and he had many friends. Not one person speaks of Jim, but what they tell of some favor or kindness he had done for them at some time or other. Greene was examined and bound over for the Grand Jury, but they took his case before the Court Commissioner, and he fixed bail at $30,000 for Greene's appearance at the November term.*

Greene and his friends have been having stories circulated in papers throughout the territory stating that the shooting was justifiable and representing Jim as a man who had killed a good many men and generally a bad character. Several home papers attempted to do the same but were quickly overhauled, as Jim's reputation here was too well established. He was the friend and counselor of everybody.

I should be glad to hear from you and also if you can suggest anything toward the prosecution. We feel like we ought to do all we possibly can to see the foul, cowardly assassin brought to justice, for if ever a man was murdered in cold blood, it was poor Jim.

The description of the killing given by Warnekros is corroborated by a letter from Lieutenant Burnett received from James F. Duncan, justice of the peace at Tombstone, before whom Greene was taken after the murder. Justice Duncan said:

It was a cold-blooded murder and premeditated. I held the inquest and also the preliminary examination. The Court Commissioner, on a writ of habeas corpus, let Greene go on $30,000 bail, furnished by men who are all right but who gave as security cattle and merchandise, which are subject to epidemic and fire. The case will come up at the November term of court if Greene can be found, of which I have my doubts. I cannot recommend any lawyer here to you; they are lawyers in name, but God keep me from ever having to employ any of them!

Greene surrendered to Chief of Police Charley Wiser, who then turned Greene over to Sheriff Scott White. Green only said, "I have no statement to make other than that man was the cause of my child being drowned." As the public's interest in the case developed, the same paper released more information two days later.

Greene, Wiser and White were close friends, and they had a shared dislike of Burnett in many ways. On July 8, 1897, the *Arizona Republican* ran a somewhat unusual article. It read:

> *Last Thursday in Tombstone, William C. Greene of the San Pedro shot and killed James C. Burnett. Mr. Greene claims that he ascertained beyond the shadow of a doubt that Burnett had occasioned the blowing up of his (Greene's) dam on the San Pedro, thereby causing a rush of water which overwhelmed and drowned his little girl and her companion Edna Cochran. Mr. Greene also claims that Burnett had at different times threatened his life. It is known that there had been ill feeling between the two men, who own neighboring ranches below Fairbank. The* Tucson Star *states that Burnett bore a bad reputation and is said to have killed several men.*
>
> *However that may be, Burnett was a man who was much given to threatening and whose name came before a good many grand juries. If Mr. Greene is able to show good reason for believing that Burnett was responsible for the blowing out of his dam and the consequent death of his child and can also show as he claims that Burnett had threatened his life, but a few minutes before the shooting there will be a strong tide of popular sentiment in favor of the defendant. His preliminary trial was set for Saturday, but on account of the illness of District Attorney English was postponed till today.*

In the subsequent circus-like trial in Tombstone, Greene was acquitted. Greene's wife, Ella, passed away in Los Angeles in 1899, unable to overcome the tragedy of losing their daughter. Following these devastations, Greene moved to Cananae, Mexico, and focused on prospecting. His hard work paid off when he unearthed copper from some abandoned mines—so much so that by 1899, he had set up the Greene Consolidated Copper Co. in New York. His copper mines in Mexico brought him vast wealth, as they were among the top producers in the United States, with a yearly output of thirty-six million tons. With constant demand on the rise, Greene soon became one of the wealthiest men in America; by 1906, he was worth over $80 million.

CHAPTER 8
WHAT ABOUT IKE?

Wyatt Earp has been a powerful symbol for Tombstone since the infamous gunfight at the O.K. Corral on October 26, 1881. The silver that once brought prosperity to this desert town has disappeared, but the city still survives due to the legend of this wild western shootout.

In the popular consciousness, the Earps have often been considered heroes, while the McLaurys and the Clantons were painted as villains. But now, these simplistic views have begun to blur at the O.K. Corral. The black hats and white hats are not so distinct anymore.

A small bronze plaque is mounted on the stucco wall surrounding the amphitheater where the shootout is reenacted daily. Nothing fancy and easy to overlook, it honors not the lawmen Wyatt Earp and Doc Holliday but Frank and Tom McLaury, two of the three men who passed away that fateful day. Beneath the oval portraits is a short but perplexing epitaph: "One owes respect to the living, but to the dead, one owes nothing but the truth."

So, to give the Clantons and the McLaurys their fair shake, I will tell their side of the story. It all started on October 27, 1880. On that day, Tombstone's Marshal Fred White mistakenly shot William "Curly Bill" Brocius. Wyatt Earp used his pistol to knock Brocius down and detained him, as well as Pony Diehl, Frank Patterson, Tom and Frank McLaury and Billy Clanton. This event triggered the first battle between the Earps and their adversaries, although contrary to what some movies have portrayed, Ike Clanton was not there.

Tombstone in 1881. *Wikimedia Commons.*

Five months later, tragedy struck the Kinnear & Co. Stage at Drew Station during a violent robbery attempt. The driver, Bud Philpot, and a passenger, Peter Roerig, lost their lives to the robbers. A posse was quickly assembled, and Luther King was apprehended from a nearby ranch that night. He admitted his involvement in the incident and named Bill Leonard, Harry Head and Jim Crane as his accomplices. Luther King was then brought back to Tombstone. However, he managed to escape shortly after arriving there. Before long, news of Doc Holliday's involvement in the robbery had swept through town.

A few days after Bud Philpot was fatally shot, Ike Clanton encountered Doc Holliday in Tombstone. Holliday asked if Ike had seen Will Leonard and his comrades, which Ike confirmed. Doc explained the events leading up to when Bud Philpot was murdered with a bullet through his heart. Holliday was certain that Ike must have heard Bill Leonard's version of the story by now. However, before Holliday had finished his narration, Ike interrupted him, asking Holliday not to tell him any more of it.

Again, some of the facts get blurred here. The Earps' side of the story is that Kate and Doc had just had another fight and the sheriff plied her with alcohol, then deceived her into signing an affidavit implicating Doc.

98

The Earp brothers, however, maintained that Doc was with them during the robbery. As soon as Kate sobered up the next morning, she withdrew her testimony and said that the sheriff had forced her to sign a paper she didn't comprehend. Of course, the Clantons' reply was that the Earps were simply covering for their friend.

Doc Holliday was apprehended in Tombstone four weeks later for allegedly menacing somebody violently. It was becoming evident that the allegations of homicide had incited his temper.

By the end of May 1881, Doc Holliday was facing indictment from a grand jury for reportedly being involved in a shooting altercation. Rumors swirled around him regarding his involvement in the stagecoach murders, but no concrete evidence had yet been found. It was clear that Holliday was getting worn down by all these accusations.

Shortly thereafter, Ike Clanton ran into Wyatt Earp in the Eagle Brewery Saloon at the corner of Allen and Fifth Streets in Tombstone. Wyatt proposed that he'd give Ike $6,000 in reward money in exchange for his assistance in finding or taking down the culprits behind the attempted stage robbery and murders. After considering it for a couple of days, Ike turned the offer down.

Eight days later, on June 9, 1881, the following article appeared in the *Daily Epitaph*. It reads:

> *What came very near being a serious shooting affray was prevented yesterday morning by the coolness and intrepidity of Virgil Earp, acting City Marshal. Ike Clanton, well-known in the San Simon and San Pedro valleys, and "Denny" McCann, a sporting man, had a difficulty in an Allen Street saloon, when the latter slapped the face of the former. Clanton went out and heeled himself, and "Denny" did the same. They met in front of Wells Fargo's office about 9 o'clock, and both drew their guns about the same time when Earp stepped between them and spoiled a good local item. They are both determined men, and but for the interference of the officer, there would doubtless have been a funeral, perhaps two.*

According to the *Arizona Daily Star* of Tucson, on June 23, 1881, Bill Leonard and Harry Head, two suspects in a stagecoach robbery, were killed by the Haslett brothers in Eureka, New Mexico. Sometime around July 10, Doc Holliday faced a murder hearing during which he provided an alibi. He claimed to have ridden to Charleston for a poker game during the stagecoach killings. His story must have been accepted, as he was acquitted and set free.

After the incident with Doc Holliday, Ike was determined to take matters into his own hands and seek justice. He knew the truth about Holliday's role in the stagecoach murders and started voicing his opinions openly. This only infuriated Holliday, making him angry and anxious at the same time.

An incident on August 1, 1881, in Skeleton Canyon represented a milestone in tensions in the area. A mule train of Mexicans was attacked, and their cargo of $4,000 in coins and bullion was stolen. Some of "Old Man" Clanton's cattle ranch workers were believed to be involved in the attack. Twelve days later, Old Man Clanton and his group were ambushed by Mexicans in Guadalupe Canyon's Animas Valley in New Mexico. William Lang, Dixie Lee Gray, Charley Snow and Jim Crane were all killed in the attack. Billy Byers and Harry Ernshaw escaped unscathed. It is speculated that the ambush was a revenge mission for the Mexicans' deaths twelve days earlier at Skeleton Canyon.

Jim Crane, the sole remaining man accused of the stagecoach murders, was snuffed out alongside Old Man Clanton in Guadalupe Canyon. This carried a significant consequence: no more possible witnesses could vouch for Doc Holliday's participation in the stagecoach killings.

In the early hours of October 26, 1881, Ike Clanton was having a late-night snack in a lunch house in Tombstone. That's when Doc Holiday came through and challenged him to go for his gun, even though Ike had none. Afterward, the Earp brothers, Virgil and Morgan, warned him, "The next time we see you, Ike, you better be armed 'cause we're gonna kill you." Later that same morning, Ike played poker with Virgil Earp.

First thing in the morning, Ike armed himself but was soon apprehended by Virgil and Morgan Earp for having firearms within city limits. He paid a fine of $27.50 to avoid further trouble and was released shortly afterward.

At half past two on October 26, 1881, one of the most famous Wild West gunfights occurred in Tombstone, Arizona's vacant lot no. 2, block 17. Billy Clanton and Tom and Frank McLaury were killed, and Virgil and Morgan Earp were severely injured, while Wyatt Earp and Doc Holliday escaped unscathed. Immediately after the smoke cleared, Ike Clanton demanded that the Earps and Holliday be arrested for murder. As he lay dying on the ground, Billy Clanton's

An unverified photograph of a young Ike Clanton, taken sometime before 1880. *Wikimedia Commons.*

last words were: "Drive the crowd away." This famous shootout is commonly remembered today as the gunfight at the O.K. Corral.

Two days after the gunfight, over two thousand people gathered in Tombstone to witness the largest funeral in the town's history. The three men, Billy Clanton and Tom and Frank McLaury, were laid to rest in Boothill Graveyard.

The next day, Wyatt Earp and Doc Holliday were apprehended for the deaths of Billy Clanton and the McLaury brothers. Morgan and Virgil Earp were not included in the arrests since they had been badly shot up and were bedridden.

From November 9 to 12, 1881, Ike gave evidence at the trial for Earp brothers and Doc Holliday on charges of murder, but by the twenty-ninth, all accusations against them had been dropped. After evaluating the case, Judge Wells Spicer determined there was no cause to proceed with a trial for the Earp brothers and Doc Holliday. He released the following statement as his conclusion:

> *In view of all the facts and circumstances of the case, considering the threats made, the character and position of the parties, and the tragical results accomplished, in manner and form as they were, with all the surrounding influences bearing upon the result of the affair, I cannot resist the conclusion that the defendants were fully justified in committing these homicides that it was a necessary act done in the discharge of official duty.*

By the middle of December 1881, some cowboys had begun a mission to take revenge. It appears that a planned attack was launched on the Benson stagecoach at Malcomb's Water Station near Tombstone, four miles away on Contention Road. It is believed this was an effort to target the Earp family and their friend John P. Clum. Before the month was through, Virgil Earp, Tombstone chief of police, was attacked on Fifth Street in Tombstone. Fortunately, he survived the ambush, though his left arm would be paralyzed for life. Ike and Phin Clanton were taken into custody for their involvement in the attack, yet they were released due to testimony from witnesses that proved they were in Charleston when it occurred.

Even though Wyatt Earp and Doc Holliday had been freed from murder charges, on February 9, 1882, Ike Clanton filed another lawsuit against them in Contention City, a few miles from Tombstone. They were again taken into custody while Virgil and Morgan Earp were still recovering from their gunfight injuries.

The defendants (the Earps and Holliday) submitted a writ of habeas corpus pleading that Judge Smith in Contention City had no right to detain them after the grand jury and Judge Spicer had thrown out the murder charges against them on November 29, 1881, in Tombstone. However, Judge Lucas ruled that Judge Smith did have the jurisdiction to take custody of them, so they were required to appear before him.

On February 15, 1882, Judge Smith moved the trial to Tombstone. That same day, Ike Clanton submitted another murder charge in Judge Lucas's court. However, the writ of habeas corpus was accepted, and the Earps and Doc Holliday were released from their imprisonment. Here is what Judge Lucas said:

> *Unless new evidence or circumstances occur subsequent to the first examination, it would only duplicate the first hearing.*

Morgan Earp was murdered on March 18, 1882, while playing pool in Tombstone's Campbell and Hatch Saloon. The event kicked off Wyatt Earp's vendetta ride, where he killed Frank Stilwell, Florentino Cruz and "Curly Bill" Brocius. Johnny Barnes would also die from gunshot wounds from this last gunfight.

At last, on July 13, 1882, a close friend and business partner of Ike Clanton's, John Peter Ringo, was discovered dead near Turkey Creek in Sulphur Springs Valley, Arizona. The cause of death appeared to be suicide.

In the wake of the gunfight at the O.K. Corral, the Clantons purchased a spot of land near Mary's ranch. Phin showed up in June 1882 and Ike in August. By 1885, both had 160-acre ranches about ten miles from Springerville on the New Mexico border; they named the combined property Cienega Amarilla. Meanwhile, their little sister Mary Elsie and her husband, Ebin Stanley, lived in Springerville. Ebin began teaming up with Ike and Phin in the cattle business.

By 1885, the Clanton gang had been joined by Lee Renfro, G.W. "Kid" Swingle, Longhair Sprague, Billy Evans and Ebin Stanley, who was married to one of Clanton's relatives. The group relocated their headquarters to their ranch in Springerville, Arizona. On November 6 that year, ranchers Isaac Ellinger and Pratt Plummer shared a meal with the Clanton brothers and Lee Renfro. After dinner, Ike, Renfro and Ellinger retired to a cabin on the Clanton property, where Renfro shot and killed Ellinger.

The account of what happened was printed in the *Epitaph* on August 6, 1887. It reads:

The readers of the Critic *will begin to think that the tragic carnival of death is holding daily sessions in the mountains on the border of Apache and Graham counties, but be that as it may, this seems to be a cold year for outlaws and murderers in this vicinity.*

By way of preface to the detailed report of the killing of that dastardly murderer Lee Renfro, which occurred on July 8 in the White Mountains in Graham County, I will briefly recount the circumstances under which Renfro murdered Isaac N. Ellinger, well known in this community: a young man of strict integrity, temperate habits and possessing all the qualities that are requisite to make a good citizen.

Sometime last fall, while Ellinger was temporarily absent from his ranch, which was situated just across the territorial line in New Mexico and known as the Cottonwood ranch, one Craig, at the instigation of Renfro, "jumped" the property. Mr. Ellinger had purchased the place more than a year previous and had made it his home and headquarters.

On or about November 6 last, he, in company with Wilds P. Plummer, went to Cienega Amarilla (the Clanton ranch), and it being about noon, Ellinger and his friend Plummer, upon the invitation of the Clantons, dismounted and took dinner. Besides these two gentlemen, there was present at the table, Ike and Phin Clanton, Lee Renfro, and Bill Jackson. While dining, the subject of the jumping of the ranch came up, but no hard words were passed. The first to finish eating were Mr. Ellinger, Ike Clanton, and Lee Renfro, who arose and passed to Phin Clanton's cabin, some ten or twelve steps distant. They had but entered the room when Renfro commenced to abuse Ellinger for something that it was reported had been said about the jumping of the ranch, at the same time picking up his six-shooter from the table and walking toward Ellinger. At this junction, Ike Clanton stepped in between them, but Renfro suddenly threw his pistol around Ike and shot Ellinger in the breast. Mr. Ellinger lived several days in great agony, suffering a thousand deaths, and died on or about the tenth day of November last. Renfro, seeing that his victim had received a mortal wound, asked for a horse, which was at once furnished by the Clantons, and Lee Renfro rode away and has been skulking in the mountains of Arizona most of the time since, a fugitive from justice, with no other company than outlaws and wild beasts.

It is strange how these kind of characters, in spite of their precautions, meet their doom. Renfro, with some of his kindred spirits, was camped in a canyon, opening out on the Rio Bonito, in the mountains on the Apache Indian reservation, on the 8th day of this month.

On this same date, a secret service officer, accompanied by three men furnished him by the agent of the San Carlos Indians, by a singular chance, happened to be hunting for stolen cattle belonging to the San Carlos Agency in the neighborhood where Renfro and his party were camped. As the officer and posse were riding across a plateau, they observed a man come out of a canyon about one hundred and fifty yards distant, on foot and in his shirt sleeves.

The officer said to two of his men, "You fellows, ride over to that man and tell him that we are from the southern country and, if possible, get him to come over here, as I want to question him about the trails." The two men rode over to the man in his shirt-sleeves and conversing with him a few moments, they together returned to where they had left the officer and his remaining companion, who in the meantime had dismounted and were pretending to be fixing their saddles. When the approaching party were within ten or fifteen paces, the secret service officer, who had his horse between him and the approaching party, recognized Renfro. He quickly stepped in front of his horse and called out, "Lee Renfro, throw up your hands!" repeating the order twice. Renfro, instead of obeying the command, attempted to pull his six-shooter when the officer fired, shooting him through the upper part of the heart and left lung. Renfro fell. The officer ran to him, and Renfro, calling him by name, asked:

"Did you shoot me for money?"

The officer replied: "No, I shot you because you resisted arrest."

Renfro then said, "I suppose it is all up with me," and asked the officer to take his watch and other effects he had on his person and send them to his brother in Cowboy, Texas, and without speaking another word, he breathed his last.

This man Renfro was an abject and servile tool of Ike Clanton, who met the same fate but a few weeks before, and they both occupy untimely graves within twenty miles of each other in the wilds of the White Mountains.

It is remarkable the swift and terrific retributions which has followed every man closely connected with the jumping of the Cottonwood ranch and the murder of Ike Ellinger.

Craig, the man who jumped the ranch, was shot and killed at Fairview, New Mexico, in a drunken wrangle over a horse race. Ike Clanton, who was present when Ellinger was shot down, followed closely in Craig's trail, leading into the dark valley of death, and now comes, on the same ghastly trail, the quaking, cringing, murderous soul of Lee Renfro, all crimson with the blood of an honored citizen, rushing headlong in quest of *the two kindred spirits, who have so shortly proceeded him into the "great unknown, that undiscovered country from hence no traveler returns."*

Thus ends the fourth act in the bloody tragedy of the murder of Isaac Ellinger. Ellinger's older brother, William Ellinger, was one of the most prominent cattlemen in the West, with ranches in several states and territories. William learned that his brother had lived four days, long enough to call the shooting "cold-blooded murder." William and Isaac were members of the Apache County Stock Association, and William had a lot of political clout.

In the first week of May 1886, gossip spread around Springerville about a supposed altercation between Ike Clanton and Pablo Romero over a card game. It was claimed that Romero had sustained a gunshot wound to the left hip, and Ike had taken a graze on one of his legs. All parties were brought before Justice Hogue on the twenty-third. There wasn't sufficient evidence to justify a trial, so the charges were dropped, and Ike was allowed to leave.

It was Christmas Day in 1886 when Billy Evans wanted to know "if a bullet would go through a Mormon" and shot Jim Hale at point-blank range. The Clantons had been suspected of stealing cattle from Springerville and smuggling them down the Blue River to Eagle Creek and southern Arizona for some time.

Two days after the incident, the Apache County treasurer's safe was discovered to have been broken into and its entire contents stolen. When Deputy Treasurer Francisco Baca was taken into custody, he explained that masked robbers had come to his house and coerced him into opening the safe. He claimed that Phin and Ike Clanton, Ebin Stanley, Lee Renfro of Springerville and Buck Henderson of St. Johns were responsible for the burglary; however, this story proved to be false, and Baca was found guilty of embezzling $11,166.54.

In April 1887, the Apache County Stock Association called on the Pinkerton detective agency to locate the wanted outlaws. They also employed Jonas "Jake" V. Brighton as their "secret service" officer. He was already a constable in Springerville and a range detective.

Not long after, Phin Clanton was taken into custody for cattle rustling and locked up in St. Johns. From May to June 1887, multiple grand jury indictments were placed on the Clantons and their associates. The charges ranged from theft of livestock to murder as a result of Isaac Ellinger's death.

Brighton tracked Clanton for three days before they encountered each other at Jim "Peg Leg" Wilson's ranch on Eagle Creek. As Brighton rode up to the scene, he recognized Clanton, who moved to flee and reach for his

A historical photo of Ike Clanton in 1881 by photographer Camillus S. Fly, Tombstone, Arizona Territory. *Wikimedia Commons.*

rifle. Brighton was faster and fired first, shooting Clanton through the side of his body. Clanton died almost immediately.

In late June 1887, a journalist who had been in contact with Brighton told the story of his arrest and shooting:

> *The next morning, while they were at breakfast, Ike Clanton came riding up to the front door. Mr. Brighton got up from the table, walked to the door, and was familiarly saluted by him. Just at this time, Mr. Miller stepped to the door, to be ready to render any assistance needed, and when Ike saw him, he wheeled his horse and attempted to get under cover of the thick cover which grows close to Wilson's home, at the same time pulling his Winchester from its scabbard. Both Brighton and Miller ordered him to halt, but instead of doing so, when about twenty yards distant where the trail took a turn to the left, he threw his rifle over his left arm, attempting to*

fire. At this instance, Detective Brighton fired, the ball entering under the left arm and passing directly through the heart and out under the right arm. Ike reeled in his saddle and fell on the right side of his horse, his rifle falling on the left. Before the fall, Brighton fired a second shot, which passed through the cantle of the saddle and grazed Ike's right leg. When Brighton and Miller walked up to where Ike lay, they found he was dead. Mr. Wilson, at whose ranch the shooting occurred, notified the nearest neighbors, and four men came over and identified the deceased and assisted in giving him as decent a burial as circumstances would admit.

Ike Clanton was forty when J.V. Brighton shot him down, leaving him to be buried without a marker along Eagle Creek. The law initially arrested Brighton for murder, but the charges were dropped later. These days, some speculate that Brighton had been hired by the local cattle company to take out suspected rustlers, while others believe he was a professional assassin.

A conflicting source stated that Clanton's body was left where it fell for several days until nearby Mormon ranchers buried him in an unmarked grave in the Mormon cemetery southeast of Eagar, Arizona, on what is today called the 26 Bar Ranch.

In late June of '96, Terry "Ike" Clanton—a descendant of the Clanton family—and former Citadel professor James A. Browning searched for clues about Ike's death. They searched the area near Eagle Creek in Greenlee County, Arizona, where they believed Ike was buried. After scouring the area, they uncovered a shallow grave under a large tree. This grave site might contain the remains of Ike Clanton. Since their discovery, Terry has tried unsuccessfully to interest Tombstone city officials in exhuming the remains and reinterring them at Boothill Graveyard.

CHAPTER 9
NOTHING BUT ASHES

Tombstone is widely known as a wild, lawless Old West town. It was notorious for its saloons, its bawdy houses and the infamous gunfight at the O.K. Corral. Many stories about Tombstone have been exaggerated thanks to Stuart Lake's book and movie adaptations from Hollywood. The thirty-second shootout in an empty lot by the O.K. Corral has made Tombstone an immortal part of history.

Despite the lawlessness that occasionally occurred in Tombstone, the population at its peak was more concerned about the threat of fire ravaging the town than any crime.

In early June 1881, Tombstone experienced its first battle with a major fire, which erupted near the Arcade Saloon located on Allen Street, four buildings east of Fifth Street on the north side of the road. A barrel of whiskey, set to be shipped away, caused the fire. It was rolled in front of the saloon, and its bung was removed so the employees could assess how much liquor remained inside. Then a bartender named Alexander attempted to insert a measurement rod into the opening, but it slipped from his grip. The bartender left the barrel and returned to get a wire to extract the gauge. When he came back, either with a cigar in his mouth or having just lit a match, the fumes from the bunghole quickly caught fire. The explosion sent fiery pieces everywhere.

The *Tombstone Epitaph* reported that the fire had already started to consume nearby buildings in less than three minutes. With a lack of tools to put out the flames, the fire spread quickly and engulfed other buildings in its path.

Firefighters and citizens alike were almost helpless in trying to contain it. Saving books, money and other treasured items from the burning buildings was the first priority, but due to the intense heat and uncontrollable flames, only part of this task could be completed.

Milt Joyce, owner of the Oriental Saloon, sprinted to his safe in a futile attempt to rescue his cash box before fleeing for his life as flames engulfed the building. Joyce could not save any of his possessions, including the $1,200 in paper money consumed by the fire. The destruction did not stop until six o'clock in the afternoon, leaving nothing except charred remains in its wake.

According to the *Tombstone Epitaph*, sixty-six businesses had been affected by this fire, which caused an estimated $175,000 in damages, with only $25,000 covered by insurance. The mountain timber and adobe bricks that were produced locally, combined with building materials brought in from Tucson, allowed for the ravaged area to be reconstructed relatively quickly.

Not long after the fire, a plan was set in motion. The Rescue Hook and Ladder Company was created on June 26, 1881, to construct a firehouse between Fifth and Sixth Streets on Toughnut Street. By August that same year, the building was finished, and a hook and ladder truck from San Francisco was acquired to equip it. To address water issues and ensure the fire department had an adequate supply of water when combating flames, the Huachuca Water Company had installed pipes and reservoirs from the Huachuca Mountains into Tombstone by July 1882.

On May 16, 1882, a disaster foreshadowed the Great Fire. It started in Mrs. Morton's home and boardinghouse on Toughnut Street between Second and Third Streets. While walking to her kitchen that evening, Morton stumbled and dropped her coal oil lamp, igniting a blaze. She yelled for help as it spread rapidly to six other buildings, including Mr. and Mrs. Grant's American Lodging House, on which they had only just paid off their mortgage. Fortunately, a local lawyer named Webster Street heard the cries from across the street and managed to help Morton out of the home before it burned down completely. Unfortunately, the fire department could not contain the flames any further.

The Great Fire of 1882 began in a Chinese laundry between Fourth and Fifth Streets on Toughnut, just south of Allen Street. Flames soon engulfed the adjoining garden behind the saloon before reaching the luxury apartments belonging to the Tombstone Club. Soon after, the Grand Hotel was ablaze, and even the wooden staircase at the back of the building was on fire.

Aftermath of the fire on May 25, 1882, that destroyed most of the western half of Tombstone. *Wikimedia Commons.*

The fire rushed up the stairs and spread to the windowsills, consuming carpets and furniture. Everything between Fourth and Fifth Streets and Allen and Toughnut Streets was reduced to ashes in less than a quarter of an hour. The firefighters decided to focus on the northern side of Allen Street to save what remained, but it quickly became impossible.

The Occidental Saloon was soon overwhelmed by the flames that spread to the Alhambra. The roaring inferno then jumped to either side, consuming the Cosmopolitan Hotel on one end and the Eagle Brewery, also known as the Crystal Palace, on the other. Fifth Street was devoured in its wake. Brown's Hotel quickly followed Hafford's Corner Saloon as the fire spread. It reached the gun store on Fourth Street, which had a considerable amount of gunpowder in its basement. Cartridges and other combustible items were stored in the shop, and soon, between the exploding cartridges and shouting people, the noise was unbearable.

The fire spread quickly to Fremont Street, engulfing everything between Fourth and Fifth Streets. The firemen successfully curtailed the flames at the corner of Fifth Street and Allen, barely saving Milt Joyce's Oriental Saloon from significant destruction. The blaze then crossed over Fourth Street, burning Levinthall's clothing house and the office of the *Nugget* newspaper.

The flames quickly spread to the neighboring buildings on the same block, consuming each one in turn. The fire then moved northward toward Fremont Street, but luckily, firefighters, police officers and citizens were able to contain it before it could do any further damage.

Based on estimates from the *Epitaph*, the damage to the town was believed to be nearly half a million dollars, and only half of that amount would be covered by insurance. Unfortunately, one death occurred during this disastrous event: the body of an unknown man was found in the back of the Cosmopolitan Hotel after the flames had been extinguished. In addition, several others were injured due to falling debris, walls collapsing or getting burned.

On receiving a donation of $180 from residents of the district to improve medical care for the firefighters, the head of the fire department declined it and sent it back with an earnest note: "Being not in need of pecuniary assistance and believing as firemen, it was our duty to accept the consequences of the fire, however serious."

On June 3, the *Epitaph* published an opinion piece that stated,

> *While the people of Tombstone sincerely thank those citizens of the territory who have proffered assistance, they wish it to be understood that they are in no need of aid. No one is suffering on account of the fire, and if there was, our citizens are both able and willing to take care of them.*

The fire station on Toughnut Street. *Library of Congress.*

And, indeed, they did just that. An article from the *Tombstone Weekly Epitaph* on July 1, 1882, spoke of the rebuilding process. The article also gives one an idea of how much damage the fire caused and how Tombstone looked after the fire.

One month ago, yesterday, the fire fiend desolated Tombstone. The heart of the city was burned out, business prostrated, and enterprise blocked. We can now even imagine the flames speeding across Allen Street and the firemen making their gallant stand at Joyce's corner. It is impossible to witness the awful scene without being impressed with the savage grandeur. Who that heard the screaming of women, that witnessed the trembling of men, and saw the lurid flames spreading havoc and destruction on that dreadful day could believe that Tombstone was possessed of such Roman firmness as to be again rebuilt one month after?

The article continues, describing the rebuilding of the "Town Too Tough to Die."

Wehrfritz, with characteristic enterprise, has re-erected his magnificent building on the corner of Fifth and Allen streets. This building, now on the eve of completion, is 30×120 feet. Eighty feet of the building, fronting on Allen Street, will be occupied by Wehrfritz himself as a beer hall and gambling saloon. It will be elegantly fitted up and furnished; a fountain erected in the center where cool water will constantly play and sportive goldfish gambol. The next compartment, on Fifth Street, at present occupied by Wehrfritz's saloon, will be used by Frank Beluda as a barber shop, and the remainder of the building on Fifth Street will be occupied by the Rockaway restaurant. The building will be completely finished by the Fourth of July and will cost $8,500.

Vicker's building is next to Wehrfritz's and is now nearly completed. This building is 30×70 and will be used by Mr. Lenoir as a furniture store. This building will cost $2,500. The next building is owned by Mr. Sampson and will be occupied by Myers, the tailor, and Duval, the assayer. This building is 27×30 feet and will be erected at a cost of $3,000.

Ritchie's building is next in line and is rapidly approaching completion. This will be a two-story building, and the ground floor has already been secured by Fitzhenry & Mansfield, the enterprising grocers. The upper story will probably be occupied by the Tombstone Club. This building is

The firehouse on Toughnut Street was constructed in response to the disastrous fires that plagued Tombstone. *Wikimedia Commons.*

22×60 and will probably cost $3,000. Fitzhenry & Mansfield have already swung out their sign to inform the public of their intended removal.

Going along Allen Street, the Alhambra saloon building, owned by Nichols & Malgren, is found hugging Wehrfritz's building on the corner. This building was first started and first completed. It is now ready for the furniture, being ceiled, painted, and prepared in fine style. It will be occupied and opened on July 01. It is elegantly furnished, is 30×80 feet, and cost not less than $5,000.

Further on, Ayimers building, 30×80, is on the high road to completion. This building will be occupied by the old tenants Campbell and Hatch. These gentlemen expect to open up their saloon about the fifteenth. Mr. Campbell has just returned from San Francisco, where he purchased a couple of billiard tables and a complete stock of fixtures. It is expected that this will be one of the finest saloons in the Territory. Robert Gray bought thirty-three feet from Bilicke by the side of the budding, and work was commenced on a building yesterday. All the above work was done by Bruce & Jones, well-known contractors, and the promptitude and workmanlike manner in which the work was performed redounds to their credit. Schmeding's building is also in a fair way of being completed in a few days.

McCoy's building is also nearly finished and will be a very tasteful structure. It is divided into two compartments, one of which will be occupied by the Baron's as a barber shop and the other by a jeweler. This building is 30×60 and will cost $3,500. A. Hill is the contractor.

114

Bilicke has not, as yet, broke ground for his hotel, though it is expected he will soon, though fears are entertained that a large building of that kind could not be finished before the advent of the rainy season.

Crossing to the south side of Allen Street, we find Mr. Comstock's building, formerly the Grand Hotel, almost ready for occupancy. The principal compartment here will be occupied by L.F. Blackburn as a saloon. There will be a bar room 42 feet in depth, with four card rooms of 12 feet square each, in the rear. Mr. Blackburn will depart for San Francisco in a few days to purchase a stock and complete set of fixtures and promises to open one of the finest saloons in town in the near future.

The other apartment lying parallel with Blackburn's will be used as a restaurant by Jakey. The basement will be used by Alderson & Grattan for their "Fountain" saloon and lunchroom. The probable cost of this building will be in the neighborhood of $10,000. The work has been done under the superintendency of Thomas Stillwell.

Mr. Solomon's building, 30×80, is also nearly completed. This will be occupied by Mr. Schoentlend and used as a furniture store. Goad & Fennell are the contractors, and the cost will be in the neighborhood of $3,000. Hietzelman & Berry's building, 30×75 feet, will be finished in a few days. It has not been decided as yet what this building will be used for. Goad and Fennell are the contractors, and they are doing their work well. Mr. A.B. Barnett's building on the corner of Allen and Fifth Streets is also nearing completion. It will be occupied by Myers Brothers, the clothes, and Cohn's tobacco and cigar store. This building is 70×30 and will cost not less than $6,000.

The Tribojett Bros. will have all their buildings ready for occupancy in about three weeks more. The first one, on the corner of Allen and Fourth Streets, is 18×60 and 15 feet high. It will be used as a saloon. The next one is the same size and will be used as a restaurant. Three other houses are 15×60 each, and one will be a beer hall, the other a butcher shop, and the third has not yet been rented. The last in the row will be 12×60 and is not rented either. The net cost will not be less than $18,000.

Fremont Street between Fourth and Fifth will soon be freed from the disfiguring marks of the great fire. Everhardy will occupy his old stalls in Spruance's building in a few days. This building is 60×30. J.H. Cummings is the contractor.

The Melrose restaurant will be completely finished in a few days and immediately occupied. This building is owned by Fred Castle, and E. Dickerson is the contractor. The building is 103×24.

Mr. Spruance, who owns much property on Fremont Street, is also building the Arcade on Allen Street. This building, when complete, will be occupied by Jack Doling as a saloon and Keno Ike in the rear. Bolan, the cigar man, will occupy another compartment. Dickerson had also the contract for putting up this building.

A.T. Otis & Co. are erecting three buildings on Fremont Street that will soon be completed. The first of these, 20×86, will be used by Otis & Co., the hardware merchants. The next, 17×56, is to rent, the third, 17×56, will be used by Mr. Gregory as a restaurant. Doremas is the contractor. These buildings will cost not less than $5,000. The large warehouse in the rear has been completed.

Robert Campbell's building on Fourth Street is nearly finished. It will be occupied as a restaurant. Cost not less than $2,500. Mr. Austin started to work on a fireproof cellar on Fremont Street, opposite the Epitaph *office, yesterday morning. Mr. Buford will commence to rebuild on the corner of Fourth and Allen in a few days, and Mr. Bauer will start to work on the corner of Fourth and Fremont about the same time.*

If the fires were not bad enough, Tombstone also had to deal with earthquakes. On May 3, 1887, the citizens of Tombstone near the Sulphur Springs Valley were shocked out of their homes. The tremors, which lasted from forty to one hundred seconds, began with a low rumble followed by two powerful shocks. Plaster and walls in buildings shifted, and some even came down, while chimneys tumbled to the ground. Inside, glassware shattered, and globes from the Crystal Palace's chandeliers fell down on patrons below them. The mines sustained minor damage, but every clock in town stopped at once. On May 4, 1887, the *Tombstone Epitaph* reported on this disaster.

Yesterday evening, just as the hands on the dial of the clock pointed to three, there was a shock of an earthquake, such as was never felt in Arizona. Notwithstanding the fact that no previous warning of its approach by prophecy or otherwise had been given, when the shock was felt, no time was lost in the vacation of the various structures of the city. Allen Street presented such an appearance of excitement as was never before witnessed. But be it said to the credit of the citizens of this city, there was less display of fear than is common on such occasions. By all who had ever experienced such shock, it was pronounced to be exceedingly severe, and to those who had never felt the quakings of Mother Earth, the half-minute's suspense was terrible. The shock lasted fully thirty seconds, during which time the

Remnants of several buildings that were damaged by the earthquake in 1887. *Library of Congress.*

trembling walls and rattling window panes furnished music dreadful but sublime in its nature. Several walls of buildings along Allen Street show evidence of the nearness of their destruction by the gaping seams left to view. And while their strength was being tested, the glassware of other places was being shaken from its position and, in many instances, falling to the floor to meet a hasty destruction.

For months after the disaster, tremors of various intensities kept reoccurring, causing some people to take refuge outside in fear of their houses crumbling. Eventually, repairs were made and the rubble cleared. The towns were restored, and tales of the blaze in the hills and the earth shaking reverberated through the years.

It took only a few short months for entrepreneurs and citizens to reconstruct Tombstone, earning it its famous nickname: the Town Too Tough to Die. The highwaymen, murderers, livestock thieves and law enforcers didn't make Tombstone live up to that slogan; the industrious businessmen and the resilient people of Tombstone did. They were the ones who rose from the ashes and went on with their lives despite what had happened.

CHAPTER 10

IN THE GUNSMOKE

Tombstone was a wild place, and gunfights happened frequently. The most renowned of these standoffs was the gunfight at the O.K. Corral in 1881. Doc Holliday and the Earp brothers clashed with a gang of outlaws, ending in three deaths. This violent encounter perfectly captured the chaotic atmosphere that defined the region.

On the evening of October 28, 1880, several Cowboys came to town and began drinking. Shots were heard from various parts of the town as they fired their revolvers in the air. Marshal White approached them and got them to surrender their weapons without incident. All of those confronted by him gave up their guns peacefully.

Later that night, White located "Curly Bill" Brocius on a deserted street in a lot where the Bird Cage Theatre is now situated. Brocius was drunk and shooting his gun randomly into the air. White asked Brocius to give him his pistol, which he accepted by passing it to White barrel-first. Wyatt Earp later said he thought the hammer had been pulled back partway over a round, though the pistol contained six live rounds. As White held onto the barrel and yanked, the weapon went off, striking White in the groin area.

In the darkness, Wyatt Earp witnessed the gun flash but did not have an unobstructed view of events. Believing Brocius was carrying a weapon, Earp struck him with his pistol, rendering him unconscious. It wasn't until after Brocius had been handcuffed by Wyatt and his brother Morgan, who were both working as Pima County sheriff's deputies, that they noticed his gun lying on the ground.

An unauthenticated photo of Curly Bill Brocius from the Bird Cage Theatre in Tombstone. *Wikimedia Commons.*

It was said that Brocius felt horrible for shooting White, whom he actually liked. The following day, Wyatt Earp and a deputy took Brocius to the county jail in Tucson to avoid a possible lynching, as Tombstone had only a feeble one-room wooden jail close to where the shooting happened.

White passed away two days after the incident; however, he was able to provide testimony before his death that exonerated Brocius. White stated that the gun went off accidentally when Brocius drew it, as he did not know it was cocked. Judge Neugass in Tucson dismissed the charge against Brocius due to White's evidence and a demonstration showing how the weapon could be fired in the half-cocked position.

Though he was sorry about the shooting of White and thankful for Earp's help in taking him away from the scene, Brocius was angry about being beaten by Earp when arrested. This caused an increase in conflict between the Earps and the Cowboys.

In Tombstone, the Bird Cage Theatre was more than just a place to watch shows; it was also a bar, a brothel and a gambling hall. People came for the lively atmosphere, but fights and killings were common occurrences that gave the theater its dark reputation as one of the most dangerous places in town. More than twenty-six deaths occurred inside the walls of the Bird Cage Theatre.

During the wild times of the territorial era, Cochise County was a rough place. Tombstone's unruly roads were a breeding ground for criminal activity, and the southern Arizona county made headlines with its stories of violence and mischievousness. The coroner's office of Cochise County, from 1880 to 1901, kept records of the various causes of death. Despite the area being mostly desert, some drownings were listed, as well as deaths caused by morphine or alcohol consumption. However, the majority of deaths were due to gun violence. A local historian estimated the death toll during this period to be 480, with 43 deaths resulting from natural causes.

The law enforcement body in Tombstone was weakened by a feud between the sheriff's office and the local deputy marshal, who also served as chief of police. In 1881, when the Cochise County and Tombstone city authorities were trying to work out their differences, the territorial governor vacated his post, and unfortunately, the president of the United States had been shot by an assassin and was lying immobile in bed.

Tombstone's weak legal system caused the practice of vigilante justice to become the norm. With limited resources and a culture of lawlessness, citizens felt obligated to bring about order in their own way. Vigilante organizations grew out of this need for swift justice, taking on roles previously held by judges and juries but without any regard for the law. Desperation drove these groups to find solutions outside of established boundaries.

Lynching as a form of vigilante justice was not unheard of, and at times, allegations alone were enough to condemn an individual regardless of innocence or guilt. This type of justice highlighted how dangerous Tombstone society was, where survival frequently hinged on people's abilities to navigate complex moral and ethical terrain. Some think vigilantes were a necessary evil due to the lack of proper legal systems. The repercussions were often dire: innocent lives were taken, and the idea of justice became distorted—with revenge taking precedence over finding out the truth— resulting in a perpetual pattern of violence and retaliation that just worsened the lawlessness the vigilante movement sought to eradicate.

Above: A group of people acting out a gunfight from the Gamblers' War in Tombstone. *Library of Congress.*

Right: Wyatt Earp at age twenty-one in 1869 or 1870, around the time he married his first wife, Urilla Sutherland. This photo was probably taken in Lamar, Missouri. *Wikimedia Commons.*

Tombstone, Arizona, was also home to a sizable Chinese population who worked in the mining and labor industries. Ethnic tensions and discrimination remained prevalent, eventually resulting in the Chinese Massacre of 1881. An angry mob of miners and other townsfolk forcefully invaded Chinatown, leading to the deaths of at least four Chinese residents and the exile of many more.

Tombstone's prosperity was interconnected with the success of its mines, yet they were hazardous places to work. Consequently, many miners died from cave-ins and accidents that happened underground. Mine owners often ignored safety precautions and exploited laborers, contributing to the town's unfortunate history.

The local newspaper, the *Tombstone Epitaph*, documented the frenzied and violent history of Tombstone, Arizona. Its dynamic headlines provided a vivid but dark depiction of the town's thriving period. The paper served as a chilling reminder of the town's violent nature and reported on its history unfiltered and unvarnished. It gave authentic insight into the lawlessness and violence that characterized the town's heyday, serving as a historical record and window into the minds of its inhabitants.

The *Arizona Star* published an interesting piece on August 27, 1880, titled "The Latest Tombstone Tragedy." This article reports that one Earp brother sent a telegram to another about a murder in Tombstone, and Wyatt Earp went after the murderer and captured him.

A telegram received from Deputy Sheriff Wyatt Earp of Tombstone by his brother informs him that a man named Malcolm was killed the night before last at the springs near Tombstone.

Earp started at once in pursuit of the murderer, who was finally captured yesterday on the San Pedro. Details of the affair, received yesterday afternoon, are to the following effect:

Mr. Malcolm kept a bar near Mineral Springs, and about 600 yards from him, another man named Mason also had a bar and a mineral well. An Italian, whose name is unknown, had left a pistol some time ago with Mason, and day before yesterday, he went to claim it.

It is said that Mason was intoxicated and refused to return the weapon, whereupon the Italian knocked him down and beat him unmercifully. Malcolm, hearing the cries for help from his neighbor, snatched up an old unloaded shotgun and started for Mason's, whom he found on the floor, and the Italian still striking him with might and main.

After attempting to pull the Italian off and failing, Malcolm struck him with the gun, which being old, broke off near the stock. The Italian then got up and inquired what business Malcolm had to interfere, to which he received the reply that he would not see his friend ill-used.

The Italian then said he was being unjustly deprived of his pistol, and Malcolm advised Mason to return it. This was done, and they all took a drink.

The Italian then suddenly turned upon Malcolm and told him to drop the stock of his gun, which he still held, and gave him a minute to do it. Almost immediately after, he shot, putting four bullets through Malcolm's body. He also fired twice at Mason, missing him, and fled to the bushes, where he was soon lost. Malcolm only lived a few minutes after the cowardly shooting.

As soon as Deputy Sheriff Earp obtained the particulars of the shooting, he started in pursuit, and after a hard chase, found the murderer near the San Pedro and brought him back to Tombstone and lodged him in jail.

On occasion, the gun violence of the territory involved anonymous people whose tales were almost lost to time. One such incident was reported by the *Tombstone Epitaph* on June 10, 1882.

Word reached town yesterday morning that a miner working about four miles from town was killed in his cabin by some unknown assailants. Word was brought to Coroner Matthews, and without unnecessary delay, that officer proceeded to the scene of the murder. The victim was partially unrecognizable and without friends interested in his fate. He was employed at the Mamie R. mine, about halfway between here and Charleston.

The superintendent of the mine is at present absent in the East, and Mr. Geo. Pridham is acting in his stead. From all we can learn from all parties who seem to know anything about the matter, the man's name was E. Brodines, a German. He bore the reputation of being a sober, steady man and had few enemies. On the first of this month, himself and a partner, who had a contract on the Mamie R, were paid off at Pridham's. A row ensued during the payment arrangements, and the partners quarreled viciously. They were ordered out of the store and, without much dalliance, obeyed the injunction. They had not been seen since by their employer.

The partner's name is Endlich. He has not been seen for a number of days, and his whereabouts is still unknown. About 3 o'clock in the afternoon, Dr. Matthews, the county coroner, accompanied by Dr. Goodfellow, the county physician, a deputy sheriff, and a reporter, repaired to the scene of the murder. The remains were too horrible to contemplate.

A cabinet photograph of Dr. Goodfellow by C.S. Fly, a noted Tombstone, Arizona Territory photographer. *Wikimedia Commons.*

They were completely putrided, and it required all the nerve of strong men to stand the stench. Dr. Goodfellow made an autopsy of the remains and found that the deceased had met his death from gunshot wounds. He must have been shot by two instruments. A shotgun loaded with heavy buckshot and a revolver must have been employed in the execution. The doctor found two buckshot and one bullet, of not less than 45 calibre, in the interior of the skull. It required all the science that medicine is master of to determine the location of the deadly missiles. The assassin must have been very near his victim when the fatal shot was fired. The bullets made an easily traceable incision in the front of the forehead and a large regular hole in the outlet in the rear. When and under what circumstances the unfortunate man was killed could not be determined yesterday, but it is hoped that at the inquest today, the whole matter will be fully brought before the light of investigation.

Six months after the famous gunfight near the O.K. Corral, the *Tombstone Epitaph* relayed another story of murder on March 27, 1882. It read:

At 2 o'clock yesterday afternoon, the jury sat upon the body of Florentine Cruz, the half-breed Indian who was found dead near Pete Spence's wood ranch, in the South pass of the Dragoons, on Thursday, the body having been brought to town and deposited at Ritter's undertaking rooms: Peter Tully, M. Gray, C.B. Noe, John M. Lee, John Kingsman, Wells Colby, T.J. Blackwood, J.R. Adams, M.H. Smith, A.C. Bilicke, Charles Brickwedel, and S.M. Barrow.

Dr. G.E. Goodfellow was the first witness examined, who testified as follows with regard to the wounds:

"I found four wounds on the body. I commenced the examination at his head and followed down. The first shot entered at the right temple, penetrating the brain; the second produced a slight flesh wound in the right shoulder; the third entered on the right side of the body, near the liver, and made its exit to the right of the spine, about five or six inches to the right. The fourth struck in the left thigh and made its exit about seven or eight inches above the point of entry. In my opinion, two of the wounds, those in the head and right side, were sufficient to cause death.

"The wound in the thigh was probably produced when he was running or after he had fallen. He was probably lying on the ground. In my opinion, he was lying on the ground, after the wounds in the upper part of the body had been received. In my opinion, the wound in the thigh was

received after he was dead. I form that opinion from the absence of blood around the wound."

In this same newspaper is an article called "The Battle of Burleigh." For those unfamiliar with this locale, it is the name of the spring where the Earps and their allies clashed with Curly Bill and the Outlaws, resulting in Curly Bill's demise. This location, also known as Iron Springs, is familiar to most Arizona history buffs. The article contains a firsthand eyewitness account of the gunfight and is quite interesting.

The town has been full of reports for the last two or three days as to the whereabouts of the Earp party and their probable movements. No sooner had one report got well underway before another was started that contradicted it. There has been marching and countermarching by the sheriff and his posse until the community has become so used to the ring of spurs and clank of steel that comparatively little attention is paid to the appearance of large bodies of horsemen in the streets. Yesterday afternoon the sheriff with a large force started down the road toward Contention, possibly to follow up the report that the party had been seen in the Whetstone mountains, west of the San Pedro River, with their horses completely fagged out, and the men badly demoralized. This, like the many other reports, was as baseless as the fabric of a dream.

Yesterday afternoon, as the sun was descending low down the western horizon, had a person been traveling on the Crystal or Lewis Spring Road toward the Burleigh Spring, as our informant was, he would have seen one of the most desperate fights between the six men of the Earp party and nine fierce cowboys, led by the daring and notorious Curly Bill, that ever took place between opposing forces on Arizona soil.

Burleigh Spring is about eight miles south of Tombstone and some four miles east of Charleston, near the mine of that name, and near the short road from Tombstone to Hereford. As our informant, who was traveling on horseback leisurely along toward the Burleigh, and as he rose a slight elevation in the road about a half mile south thereof, he observed a party of six men ride down to the spring from the east, where they all dismounted, they had not much more than got well upon their feet when there rose up at a short distance away, nine armed men who took deadly aim and fired simultaneously at the Earp party, for such the six men proved to be. Horrified at the sight, that like a lightning stroke flashed upon his vision, he instinctively stopped and watched for what was to follow. Not a man went down under this murderous fire, but like a thunderbolt shot from the hand of Jove, the six desperate men charged upon their assailants like the light brigade at Balaklava, and when within easy reach returned the fire under which one man went down never more to rise again. The remaining eight fled to the brush and regained their horses when they rode away toward Charleston as if the King of Terrors was at their heels in hot pursuit. The six men fired but one volley, and from the close range, it is supposed that several of the ambushed cowboys were seriously, if not fatally, wounded.

The six men returned to their horses, where one was found to be in the agony of death, he having received one of the leaden messengers intended for his rider. The party remained at the spring for some time, refreshing themselves and their animals when they leisurely departed, going southerly as if they were making for Sonora.

After the road was clear, our informant rode on and came upon the dead man, who, from the description given, was none other than Curly Bill, the man who killed Marshal White in the streets of Tombstone one year ago last September. Since the above information was obtained, it has been learned that during the night, the friends of Curly Bill went out with a wagon and took the body back to Charleston, where the whole affair has been kept a profound secret so far as the general public is concerned.

Of course, the reason for this confrontation was the murder of Wyatt Earp's younger brother Morgan. After the famous gunfight, the Earps, in search of security, checked into the Cosmopolitan Hotel and recruited several bodyguards to supplement their protection.

Two months following the shootout at the O.K. Corral, in December 1881, Virgil Earp was severely wounded during an assassination attempt—leaving him with a permanently damaged left arm. His brother Morgan grew anxious about their safety in Tombstone and sent Louisa, his wife, to stay with his parents in Colton, California. He stayed behind to help take care of his brothers.

Morgan had just come back from a musical performance at Schieffelin Hall on the evening of Saturday, March 18, 1882. He was in the middle of playing a game of billiards against Bob Hatch, the owner of Campbell and Hatch Billiard Parlor. Dan Tipton, Sherman McMaster and Wyatt were all present as well. Wyatt had also been given warnings earlier that very same day. Suddenly, Morgan was ambushed.

Morgan was shot through the top pair of windows on a four-pane windowed door leading to an alley between Allen and Fremont Streets. The

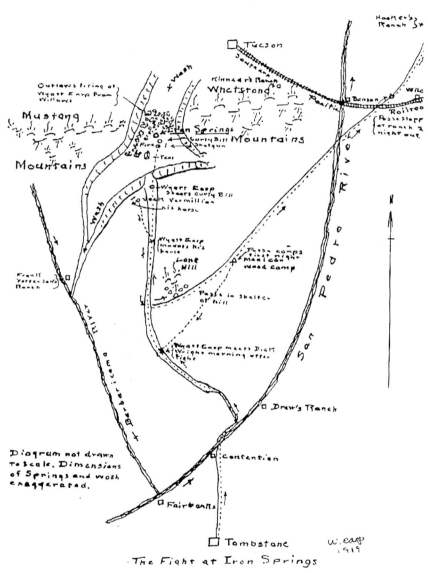

During 1918 and 1919, Wyatt Earp told his story about the Gunfight at the O.K. Corral and its aftermath to John Flood. With Earp's input, Flood drew a map of the location of Iron Springs, where Earp killed Curly Bill Brocius. *Wikimedia Commons.*

other two panes had been painted over. He stood about ten feet away from the door when a bullet struck him in the back, traveled through his body and lodged in George A.B. Berry's thigh. Another projectile smashed into the wall above Wyatt's head. Men ran into the alley, but it was already too late. The gunman had fled.

When Morgan was shot, his brothers tried to help him get up, but he said no. "Don't, I can't stand it. This is the last game of pool I'll ever play."

He was brought to a spot close to the entrance of the card room. First to come was Dr. William Miller, followed by Drs. Matthews and Goodfellow. The medical team studied Morgan. Goodfellow, who would one day become renowned in the United States for treating abdominal gunshot wounds, determined that Morgan's injuries were fatal. Goodfellow described Morgan's wounds:

> *He was in a state of collapse resulting from a gunshot, or pistol wound, entering the body just to the left of the spinal column in the region of the left kidney emerging on the right side of the body in the region of the gall bladder. It certainly injured the great vessels of the body, causing hemorrhage, which undoubtedly causes death. It also involved the spinal column. It passed through the left kidney and also through the loin.*

Stuart Lake wrote in *Wyatt Earp: Frontier Marshal* that as Morgan was on the brink of death, he uttered to Wyatt, "I can't see a damned thing." Wyatt mentioned that he and Morgan had both agreed to share their visions of the afterlife once they were close to death. Morgan was then moved to a comfortable setting, where his family—Wyatt, Virgil, James, Allie and Bessie—all gathered around him. Morgan died less than an hour after he was shot.

Morgan was dressed in Doc Holliday's blue suit after he passed away, and his memorial service was held at the Cosmopolitan Hotel. When Wyatt heard that Frank Stilwell and other outlaws were lying in wait for them in Tucson, he quickly gathered some deputies to protect Virgil, Maddie, Ally and James.

The Earps took Morgan's body to Benson in a wagon, then hired another one for the long journey from Benson to Contention, where they caught a train to Tucson. As they waited for the next departure, the Earps saw Stilwell lurking and shot him dead. James and Virgil traveled with Maddie, Ally and Morgan's coffin to Colton, California, where the deceased's wife and parents were waiting. Morgan was initially buried near Mount Slover in the old city cemetery of Colton. When this cemetery was moved in 1892, his remains were reinterred down the road in Hermosa Cemetery.

As Wyatt and James transported Morgan's corpse to Contention, Dr. D.M. Matthews, the coroner, set up a coroner's jury to investigate his death. Marietta Duarte, Pete Spence's wife, was willing to testify to the jury; her husband mistreated her and had a reason to incriminate him. She accused her spouse and four other men of murdering Morgan.

Duarte took the stand and testified that her spouse had been out on the porch with Indian Charlie the day before when they spotted Morgan Earp passing by. Pete Spence pointed at him and said to Charlie, "That's him; that's him." The Indian then marched forward to get a better look at Earp. Spence was not home the night of the shooting, but around midnight, Cruz

A photograph of Morgan Earp taken before he arrived at Tombstone. *Wikimedia Commons.*

and Frank Stilwell came by, each armed with a gun and a carbine. Shortly after, Frederick Bode and another unknown individual, later identified as Hank Swilling, showed up. Both had rifles, and they conversed in hushed tones. The following morning, Spence struck Marietta and her mother and threatened to shoot Marietta if she revealed what had happened. Witnesses reported seeing Frank Stilwell running from the scene.

The coroner's jury determined that Morgan Earp came to his death in the city of Tombstone on March 18, 1882, because of a gunshot or pistol wound inflicted at the hands of Pete Spence, Frank Stilwell, a party by the name of Freis and two Indian half-breeds, one of whom was named Charlie. Still, the name of the other was not ascertained.

When the prosecution summoned Marietta Duarte to provide testimony at the preliminary hearing, the defense objected due to her statements being considered hearsay and the fact that a spouse could not be obligated to offer evidence against their partner. The judge agreed with this explanation and dismissed the case. Despite being the sheriff of Cochise County, Behan and his deputies did not make a substantial effort to apprehend Morgan Earp's killers.

Earp's vendetta ride aside, a large number of outlaws still frequented Tombstone. Cochise County deputy sheriff Billy Breakenridge had some strong words about Zwing Hunt, one of the most notorious outlaws in that unruly county. Originally from Texas, Hunt had come from a good background, but something changed him for the worse.

Hunt and his friend Billy Grounds rode into Arizona, where Hunt worked as a ranch hand before venturing into criminal activity. The pair began stealing livestock but stepped it up by ambushing a caravan carrying silver bullion and coins in Skeleton Canyon. Once the deed was done, they buried the loot inside the canyon and disappeared without a trace. To this day, Skeleton Canyon is full of legends and stories about the infamous lost treasure.

Supposedly, Zwing and Billy had more Mexican adventures. As revealed by Zwing on his deathbed, they allegedly escaped from Mexico after three months of raiding with two four-horse wagons full of spoils. Their company was an unsavory group that featured Johnny Ringo, Curly Bill Brocius, Tom and Frank McLaury and the notorious Clantons.

In the autumn of 1881, thirty cows were taken from Sulphur Springs Valley and moved to Charleston along the San Pedro River. The descriptions of the perpetrators seemed to point to Zwing Hunt and Billy Grounds as the culprits. Before the authorities could apprehend them, they had already fled into Mexico.

The following year, two figures shrouded in masks and armed with rifles infiltrated the Tombstone Mining Company's office. In an instant, they shot M.R. Peel, the chief engineer, and vanished into the night as suddenly as they had come. It was speculated that they intended to commit a heist, but one accidentally discharged his weapon.

Several days later, news went to the sheriff's station in Tombstone that Zwing Hunt and Billy Grounds had taken refuge at the Chandler Ranch, some nine miles away from the town.

Sheriff John Behan was away with another posse, so Deputy Billy Breakenridge took charge of apprehending the criminals. He recruited a posse of five people and galloped to the ranch, arriving just before daybreak on March 29, 1882.

Breakenridge split his men into two groups: Jack Young and John Gillespie were assigned to watch the back entrance of the ranch house, while Hugh Allen and himself kept an eye on the front. Yearning for glory, Gillespie marched up to the door and pounded it heavily, proclaiming, "It's me: the sheriff!"

As soon as the door opened, Gillespie was instantly killed by a gunshot. Another bullet pierced Young's thigh.

Just as the door opened, a gunshot hit Allen in the throat, sending him to the ground. Breakenridge yanked Allen by his shirt and dragged him away before diving behind a tree when another shot whizzed past them. The shooter then stepped into view, ready to fire again. Breakenridge pulled his shotgun up and fired, hitting Billy straight in the face. The outlaw crumpled to the ground, fatally wounded.

On regaining consciousness, Allen quickly grabbed a rifle as Zwing Hunt appeared. Breakenridge and Allen began shooting, aiming for the outlaw's chest. In two minutes, this gun battle resulted in two fatalities and three injured men. The deceased and injured were placed in a milk wagon and transported to Tombstone.

Though still injured, Zwing Hunt fled when his brother, Hugh, arrived from Texas. Hugh would later insist that Zwing had been killed by Apache Indians; others alleged he had returned to Texas where, on his deathbed, he sketched a map indicating the hiding place of the outlaws' treasure.

It seems that back in Tombstone's heyday, even your choice of clothing could get you into a fight. On July 24, 1880, while in Corrigan's saloon, Tom Waters was subjected to a few jests from his comrades regarding his black-and-blue plaid shirt. After a good amount of time had passed, Tom felt that the jokes had run their course and declared loudly, "I'll knock down any man who opens his mouth about my shirt again!"

Tom's friend E.L. Bradshaw stumbled into the saloon shortly after his proclamation and commented about the flashy new article of clothing. True to form, Tom knocked him out and exited the building, leaving Bradshaw unconscious on the floor.

An injured and livid Bradshaw confronted Tom near Vogan's Alley afterward, demanding to know why he was hit. After all the jokes directed toward him, Tom, very drunk and hostile, retorted with a raging verbal assault. In response, Bradshaw fired multiple shots at Tom: one penetrated his left arm and entered his heart, another struck his head and two more hit his back. Although he stood trial for shooting Waters, Bradshaw was ultimately declared not guilty.

The following day, July 25, 1880, the *Tombstone Epitaph* published this account of the Waters shooting.

> *About 7 o'clock last evening, the pistol was used with fatal effect on Allen Street, resulting in the death of T.J. Waters from gunshot wounds from a weapon in the hand of E.L. Bradshaw. The causes which led to this unfortunate tragedy are brief. Waters was what is considered a sporting man and has been in Tombstone for several months. He was about forty years of age, with a powerful build, stood over six feet in height, and weighed*

about 190 pounds. When sober, he was a clever sort of man but quite the opposite when under the influence of liquor. Yesterday, he won considerable money and had been drinking a great deal, hence was in a mood to be easily irritated. Bradshaw was an intimate friend of Waters but a very different character, being a man of medium size, over fifty years of age, and very reserved and peaceable in his disposition. We understand that these two men had prospected together, and when Waters first came to Tombstone, he lived in Bradshaw's cabin. Yesterday morning, Waters purchased a blue and black plaid shirt, little dreaming that the fated garment would hurl his soul into eternity before the sun had set. It so happened that several good-natured remarks were made about the new shirt during the day until Waters had taken sufficient liquor to make the joking obnoxious to him, and he began to show an ugly resentment and was very abusive, concluding with, "Now, if anyone don't like what I've said let him get up, God dam him. I'm chief. I'm boss. I'll knock the first son of a bitch down that says anything about my shirt again."

This happened in the back room at Corrigan's saloon, and as Waters stepped into the front room, Bradshaw happened in and, seeing what his friend was wearing, made some pleasant remark about it, whereupon Waters, without a word, struck Bradshaw a powerful blow over the left eye which sent him senseless to the floor. Waters then walked over to Vogan & Flynn's to see, as he said, "if any son of a bitch there didn't like this shirt." He had just entered the street when Ed Ferris made some remark about the new shirt, which Waters promptly resented in his pugilistic style.

After some more rowing, Waters went back to Corrigan's saloon. As soon as Bradshaw recovered from the knockdown, he went into the back room, washed off the blood, went down to his cabin, put a bandage on his eye, and put his pistol in his pocket. He then came up to Allen Street and took his seat in front of Vogan & Flynn's saloon. Seeing Waters in Corrigan's door, Bradshaw crossed towards the Eagle Brewery and walking down the sidewalk until within a few feet of Waters, said: "Why did you do that?" Waters said something, whereupon Bradshaw drew his pistol and fired four shots, all taking effect. One under the left arm probably pierced the heart, two entered above the center of the back between the shoulders, and one in the top of the head ranged downward toward the neck, any one of which would probably have resulted fatally. Waters fell at the second shot and soon expired. Bradshaw was promptly arrested, and examination will be had in the morning before Justice Gray.

Tom Waters is buried in the Boothill Graveyard just outside town, along with many others mentioned in this book. In the words of the English philosopher Thomas Hobbes:

> *Whatsoever, therefore, is consequent to a time of war, where every man is enemy to every man, the same consequent to the time wherein men live without other security than what their own strength and their own invention shall furnish them withal. In such condition, there is no place for industry… no knowledge of the face of the earth, no account of time, no arts, no letters, no society, and which is worst of all, continual fear and danger of violent death; and the life of man, solitary, poor, nasty, brutish, and short.*

BIBLIOGRAPHY

American Cowboy Chronicles. "Ike Clanton's Unedited Statement in the Preliminary Hearing Before Judge Wells Spicer." July 21, 2021. http://www.americancowboychronicles.com/2021/07/ike-clantons-unedited-statement-in.html.

———. "OK Corral Gunfight—The Tombstone *Nugget*, October 27th, 1881." August 30, 2016. http://www.americancowboychronicles.com/2016/08/ok-corral-gunfight-tombstone-nugget.html.

———. "Old West Hangings—Dancing on Air." March 10, 2016. http://www.americancowboychronicles.com/2016/03/old-west-hangings-dancing-on-air.html.

———. "The *Tombstone Epitaph*, Leslie's Luck, Nov. 18, 1882." October 14, 2015. http://www.americancowboychronicles.com/2015/10/the-tombstone-epitaph-leslies-luck.html.

Arizona State Archives. "Bisbee Arizona, Tax Roll 1888 Tombstone Arizona."

———. "Inquest Held by Justice of the Peace, Township One, Cochise County—M.D. Shearer."

———. "Phoenix Arizona, Coroner's Inquest George Daves."

Bell, Bob Boze, Gary Roberts, Jeff Morey, Casey Tefertiller and John Boessenecker. "Did Doc Kill Ringo?" *True West*, January 21, 2022. https://truewestmagazine.com/article/did-doc-kill-ringo/.

Christensen, D.T. "Was Ike Clanton Really the Loudmouth Coward of Tombstone?" OldWest, last updated November 8, 2023. https://www.oldwest.org/ike-clanton-tombstone/.

Cornish Bird. "The Murder of Billy Kinsman—Cornishman Shot Dead in Tombstone." https://cornishbirdblog.com/murder-of-billy-kinsman/. Accessed September 5, 2023.

Eppinga, Jane. "A Case of Territorial Voter Fraud." *Arizona Capitol Times*, January 27, 2013. https://azcapitoltimes.com/news/2013/01/27/a-case-of-territorial-voter-fraud-in-arizona/.

Goff, John. *Arizona Territorial Officials*. Asheville, NC: Black Mountain Press, 1975.

Herald/Review. "Who Killed Johnny Ringo?" April 27, 2016. https://www.myheraldreview.com/news/who-killed-johnny-ringo/article_0419b66c-0cd0-11e6-8094-63edd32e8c67.html.

HistoryNet Staff. "Twenty-Four Hours with Ike Clanton." August 14, 2006. https://www.historynet.com/twenty-four-hours-with-ike-clanton/.

Hobbes, Thomas. "Thomas Hobbes, *Leviathan* (1651) [Extract]." Carnegie Mellon University in Qatar. https://web2.qatar.cmu.edu/~breilly2/18th/absolutism. Accessed December 15, 2023.

Hufford, Deborah. "The True Story of Katie Elder." *Notes from the Frontier*, December 2, 2019. https://www.notesfromthefrontier.com/post/the-true-story-of-katie-elder.

"Johnny Ringo." https://www.angelfire.com/co4/earpgang/ringodeath.html. Accessed August 15, 2023.

Las Cruces Blog. "Death of Johnny Ringo—King of the Cowboys." October 21, 2015. https://lascrucesblog.com/history/2015/death-of-johnny-ringo-king-of-the-cowboys/.

Marks, Paula Mitchell. *And Die in the West: The Story of the O.K. Corral Gunfight*. Norman: University of Oklahoma Press, 1996.

McGahey, Terry. "Tombstone's Baptism of Fire, 1881 & 1882." December 19, 2016. http://www.americancowboychronicles.com/2016/12/tombstones-baptism-of-fire-1881-1882.html.

Murphy, Pauline. "The Cork Man Hanged in the Wild West for the Famous Bisbee Massacre." IrishCentral, August 16, 2023. https://www.irishcentral.com/roots/history/dan-kelly-brisbee-massacre.

Rose, John D. "Jim Burnett, a Judge on the Take, at Charleston Arizona." Wyatt Earp Explorers. https://www.wyattearpexplorers.com/jim-burnett.html. Accessed September 5, 2023.

Seibel Family Stories. "Luke Short and Hattie Buck." https://www.seibelfamily.net/luke-short.html.

Self, George. "James Burnett's Death." Tombstone Silver. https://www.tombstonesilver.com/james-burnett-death.html. Accessed September 4, 2023.

Spartacus Educational. "Virgil Earp." https://spartacus-educational.com/WWearpV.htm. Accessed September 2, 2023.

TombstoneArizona.com. "Joseph Ike Clanton." http://clantongang.com/oldwest/gangike.html. Accessed August 18, 2023.

Trimble, Marshall. "Little Gertie the Gold Dollar Was a Feisty Entertainer." *North Valley Magazine*, February 7, 2022. https://northvalleymagazine.com/little-gertie-the-gold-dollar-was-a-feisty-entertainer/.

———. "The Outlaw King of Galeyville." *True West*, July 7, 2017. https://truewestmagazine.com/article/the-outlaw-king-of-galeyville/.

———. "Zwing Hunt." *True West*, May 21, 2019. https://truewestmagazine.com/article/zwing-hunt/.

Wikipedia. "Fred White (Marshal)." https://en.wikipedia.org/wiki/Fred_White_(marshal). Accessed September 8, 2023.

———. "Gunfight at the O.K. Corral." https://en.wikipedia.org/wiki/Gunfight_at_the_O.K._Corral. Accessed August 12, 2023.

———. "Ike Clanton." https://en.wikipedia.org/wiki/Ike_Clanton. Accessed August 18, 2023.

———. "John Clum." https://en.wikipedia.org/wiki/John_Clum. Accessed September 3, 2023.

———. "Johnny Ringo." https://en.wikipedia.org/wiki/Johnny_Ringo. Accessed August 16, 2023.

———. "Morgan Earp." https://en.wikipedia.org/wiki/Morgan_Earp. Accessed September 8, 2023.

———. "O.K. Corral (Building)." https://en.wikipedia.org/wiki/O.K._Corral_(building). Accessed August 12, 2023.

———. "Shootout at Wilson Ranch." https://en.wikipedia.org/wiki/Shootout_at_Wilson_Ranch. Accessed September 6, 2023.

———. "Ten Percent Ring." https://en.wikipedia.org/wiki/Ten_Percent_Ring. Accessed September 1, 2023.

INDEX

ABOUT THE AUTHOR

Cody Polston is an amateur historian who enjoys providing guided tours of Albuquerque and other ancient places in the American Southwest. He has been featured on numerous radio and television programs, such as *Dead Famous* (Biography Channel), *Weird Travels* (Travel Channel) and *In Her Mother's Footsteps* (Lifetime Channel exclusive), as well as *Extreme Paranormal* and *The Ghost Prophecies* (both A&E Network). Cody has written numerous books on the history of the Southwest, ghost stories, paranormal fiction and fantasy.

Visit us at
www.historypress.com
....